DOMINO
KNITTING

Vivian Høxbro

Translated by Carol Huebscher Rhoades

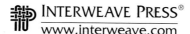

INTERWEAVE PRESS®
www.interweave.com

Translation: Carol Huebscher Rhoades
Design and Layout: Dean Howes
Charts and Drawings: Vivian Høxbro
Photography: Bjørn Jakobsen

 Interweave Press
201 East Fourth Street
Loveland, Colorado 80537
USA
www.interweave.com

Printed and bound in China through Asia Pacific Offset

Library of Congress Cataloging-in-Publication Data

Høxbro, Vivian.
    Domino knitting / Vivian Høxbro.
        p. cm.
Includes index.
    ISBN 1-931499-11-X
    1. Knitting. 2. Knitting—Patterns. I. Title.
    TT820 .H815 2002
    746.43'20432—dc21

                                    2002005720

10 9 8 7 6 5 4 3 2

Thank you to all those who have knitted the pieces for the book and to my friends who served as photo models. Thanks also to Masai Clothing for kindly loaning the garments for the photographs.

CONTENTS

BY SUBJECT

WHAT IS DOMINO KNITTING?

IN 1993, I WAS ATTENDING a handcraft fair in Germany and noticed a huge crowd at one stand. I could just barely see a bearded man demonstrating a different way to knit. That man was Horst Schulz. Later, I travelled to Berlin and took a course with him. It was on "the new knitting" as he called it, and was lively and enthralling. The Danish knitting guild, Gavstrik, sponsored a contest to select a name for the technique. The winner was "Domino Knitting," a fine and amusing name which has stuck.

In domino knitting, pieces are knitted together while the work progresses, just as one "pieces" the tiles in dominoes. For more than a century, people have knitted this way. They knitted shawls with domino patterns on the Faroe Islands and pieced coverlets in the same manner in Canada and England. In the United States, I found a copy of a pamphlet from 1946 with the sweetest jacket, knitted in domino squares by Virginia Woods Bellamy. In 1952, she published a book on the technique, called *Number Knitting.*

From the first moment I saw the domino knitting techniques demonstrated, I was intrigued by the many possibilities of this knitting method. I have worked with domino knitting in a simple, Nordic way and feel that it is very important that the garments I make will be comfortable to wear and will look nice with simple accessories.

Domino knitting is not as stressful on the knitter's arms and shoulders as other kinds of knitting. Domino is knitted on short, preferably wooden, needles or circular needles, and you knit with only a few stitches at a time. Even if you are knitting a large blanket, you only turn the short needles and the little section you are working on when you shift from right to wrong side.

There is no getting away from the fact that domino knitting is slower but who says that we have to knit quickly? We knit for the sake of enjoyment today, don't we? Who wants something fun to end quickly? Not I!

With this book, I hope to share my enthusiasm with everyone who would like to partake of it. It is so much fun to knit small pieces with short needles and to see the work growing up and out. Domino knitting's possibilities are endless. But wait! Once you're hooked, you're caught. Domino knitting is addictive.

Vivian Høxbro

TOOLS FOR DOMINO KNITTING

Be kind to yourself—only the best equip-
ment is good enough!

Needles

A pair of domino needles is absolutely
indispensable. The needles are only about
8" (20 cm) long, with a knob on one end,
so that the needle ends won't get stuck in
your clothes or your knitting. You can
buy them (see Yarn, page 84) or you can
use double-pointed needles with a bead
tightly fastened onto one end of each. My
needles are rosewood, a wonderful, flexi-
ble wood which the stitches glide across.
You will also need a circular needle and a
short needle (use a wooden needle about
4" [10 cm] long or a cable needle) for
crossing the cables.

Why domino needles? With long

needles, you use more arm movement
when turning the work. With short
needles, you reduce this movement to a
minimum.

Other Things You Will Need

Stitch markers, blunt tapestry needles,
some safety pins, measuring tape, a cable
needle, cotton tacking thread, a crochet
hook, scissors, and a pen are all useful
items to have on hand. If you are following
a chart or diagram for the knitting, you
can make a photocopy, cut out the chart
and put it with the other things. Keep it
neat and handy in a plastic sleeve so it is
easy to carry around.

On page 84, you can read about yarn
and gauge.

LEARN WHILE YOU KNIT

POTHOLDERS AND HEADBANDS

L earning doesn't need to be boring. In this section, you will be introduced to the techniques of domino knitting while you knit the festive potholders made with squares and strips, a smart turban, or a headband for yourself or a lucky child in the family.

Then, you are "educated" and can forge ahead with larger projects, working either from your own imagination or from the patterns in the book.

You don't need to knit all the potholders. The section, "Technique," in each pattern tells you which potholder demonstrates the techniques needed for that pattern.

If the pattern refers to a potholder you haven't knitted yet, you should do it before you begin the larger piece.

Potholders 1–4 show how you knit squares and how you knit them together.

Turban/Headband shows how squares are knitted together in a ring.

Potholders 5–8 show how strips are knitted together.

Borders: Each of the eight potholders has its own border which can be used on many other items.

Enjoy!

1

BASIC SQUARES

*T*hese squares are the starting point for many wonderful hours of knitting, so ready, set, go! Here you have instructions for nine different squares. The first is explained completely; the other squares are variations of the first. Knit squares 1 and 2 plus one or more of the others, so that you'll understand how they work. Then you will be ready to continue by learning how to join the squares while you knit.

Yarn: Use what you have on hand. The squares in the photos are knitted with a thick cotton yarn, "Paris" from Garn-studio.

Colors: For these squares, I've used curry, orange, rust, pink, burgundy, and red-violet.

Needles: Dn (or dpn) in a size suitable for the yarn.

Technique: Basic Squares 1–9.

Number of stitches: 25.

Basic Square 1

Garter stitch, single color
Color: Curry.

This square is a simple, garter stitch square. For abbreviations, see page 87. K-CO (page 4) 25 sts on dn (= domino needles)

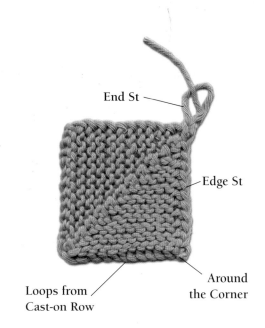

End St

Edge St

Around the Corner

Loops from Cast-on Row

Row 1 (WS): Knit to the last st, p1. Mark the center 3 sts.
Row 2 (RS): (NOTE: The yarn tail hangs at the right side). Sl 1 kwise, knit to marker before center 3 sts (= k10), sl 1 kwise, k2tog, psso, knit to the last st (= 10 sts), p1 (= 23 sts).
Row 3 and all wrong side rows: Sl 1 kwise, knit to last st, end p1.
Row 4: Sl 1 kwise, knit to marker before center 3 sts (= k9), sl 1, k2tog, psso, knit to last st (= k9), end p1 (= 21 sts).
Row 6: Sl 1 kwise, knit to marker before center 3 sts (= k8), sl 1, k2tog, psso, knit to last st (= k8), p1 (= 19 sts).
Row 8: Sl 1 kwise, knit to marker before center 3 sts (= k7), sl 1, k2tog, psso, knit to last st (= 7 sts), p1 (= 17 sts).

Continue in this manner until 3 sts remain.

Next row (WS): Sl 1 kwise, k1, p1.

Next row: Sl 1, k2tog, psso (= 1 st).

Cut yarn and pull the tail through the stitch but do not pull it tight. This last stitch is a "reuseable" stitch which will be used again when the squares are knitted together. It is called an "end stitch" (end st). The first end is not woven in. The instructions for Basic Square 2 tell you when you should weave in the ends while knitting (see page 6). This way of weaving in the ends will be revolutionary for you if you haven't done it this way before. In the next squares, most of the tails are woven in while you knit.

Basic Square 2

Garter stitch, 2 colors, striped

Colors: Rust and pink.

This square is similar to the first one except that it is striped. K-CO and knit the first row with rust (the color which is listed first), and continue knitting the

square, alternating 2 rows rust with
2 rows pink.

Weave the tails in while you work,
doing it first on Row 2 where the rust CO
tail is knitted in. The pink tail can be
woven in on Row 4 (weave in the tails,
using the method explained on page 6).

NOTE: On the right side of the square,
you can carry the yarn up between color
changes. Be sure that the yarns are not
pulled too tightly or the square will be
distorted.

Basic Square 3

Garter stitch with a "wing"
Colors: Burgundy and curry.
Knit as for Basic Square 1, with

Knitted Cast-On (K-C0)

Start with a slip st which will be the first
st. We'll call this the beginning stitch
(beg st).

Hold the ndl with beg st in the left hand
and hold an empty ndl in the right hand.

Knit 1 st into beg st, but leave beg st on left ndl.

Turn the new st and place it back onto left ndl beside beg
st (= 2 sts).

Knit into the first st on the left ndl (the new
st) in the same way, turn it, and place it on left
ndl (= 3 sts). Continue in the same manner
until you have the desired number of stitches.
When you work the knitted cast-on, you
need a beginning stitch which can be a stitch made with a slip stitch (see above)
or it can be an end st from another square or a loop (beg st) somewhere in the
work. This method of casting on is especially suitable for casting on at the end
of a row or later, when one picks up and knits sts in the CO row, because the sts
have obvious loops into which one can easily insert the needle.

burgundy except for Rows 2 and 3 which are knitted with curry.

Basic Square 4

Garter stitch with a square "spot"
Colors: Red-violet and orange.

Knitted as for Basic Square 1 with red-violet until there are 7 ridges on RS. Change to orange on RS and knit the rest of the square with orange.

Basic Square 5

Alternately stockinette and garter stitch, 2 colors
Colors: Curry and rust.

K-CO 25 sts with curry.

Row 1 (WS): Curry. Knit to the last st, p1. Mark the center 3 sts.

Row 2 (RS): Rust. Sl 1 kwise, knit to the center 3 sts (= K10), sl 1, k2tog, psso, knit to the last st(= k10), p1 (= 23 sts).

Row 3: Rust. Sl 1 kwise, purl to end of row.

Row 4: Curry. Sl 1 kwise, knit to the center 3 sts (= k9), sl 1, k2tog, psso, knit to the last st (= K9), p1 (= 21 sts).

Row 5: Curry. Sl 1 kwise, knit to the last st, p1.

Row 6: Rust. Sl 1 kwise, knit to center 3 sts (= k8), sl 1, k2tog psso, knit to last st (= k8), p1 (= 19 sts).

Row 7: Rust. Sl 1 kwise, purl to end of row.

Continue, alternating 2 garter st rows with curry and 2 stockinette rows with

End Stitch (end st)

The last stitch is a chapter in itself. I suggest that you do it this way:

1. When you are continuing with a square in the same color: Do not BO the last st (end st) but use it as the first stitch in the next square and continue knitting with the yarn (end st-1).

2. When you are continuing with a square in another color: Do not BO the last st (end st) but use it as the first stitch in the next square. Do not cut yarn until you have woven it in (end st-2).

3. When the square is finished but you are going to knit with the end st later: Cut yarn and pull it through the st but do not pull it tight (end st-3).

4. When the square is finished and it won't be used as for those above, BO the last st and cut yarn (end st-4).

rust (as for Rows 4–7), with a decreasing number of sts, until 3 sts remain.
Next row: Sl 1 kwise, p2.
Next row: Sl 1, k2tog, psso (= 1 st).

Cut yarn, pull the tail through the last st but do not pull tight.

Basic Square 6

Alternating stockinette and garter stitch, single color
Color: Pink.

Knitted as for Basic Square 5 but in one color.

Weaving in Yarn Tails

You can fasten off yarns by weaving in the tails while knitting on the right side. The woven-in yarns lie on the wrong side and are not visible on the right side. Hold the work with the yarn over the finger with which you knit multi-color patterns. The "old" color (O, white in the drawings), lies over one finger, the index finger, below the fingernail. Hold the "new" color ("N," gray in the drawings), which is the yarn you are knitting with, closer to the end of the finger and over both index and middle fingers.

*Insert ndl under O and knit 1 st with N.

Then bring the ndl over O and knit 1 st with N. Repeat from * a few times. Weave in as many tails as possible in this way, so that you won't have to darn in as many ends with a needle afterwards. Now it isn't any problem at all to knit with many colors. It is difficult to weave in tails when knitting on the wrong side, so don't try it. You can darn those tails in later with a tapestry needle.

NOTE: Always weave in the tail which is hanging the lowest down. When that is done, weave in the one which is now hanging lowest, etc.

Basic Square 7

2 color variation
Colors: Red-violet and curry.

Knit as for Basic Square 1 with red-violet until there are 5 ridges on RS. Then work 2 rows stockinette with curry (the 1st row is knitted on RS); 2 knit rows with red-violet, 2 stockinette rows with curry and the rest of the square is knitted (garter st) with red-violet. At the same time, the center 3 sts are worked sl 1, k2tog, psso on all right side rows.

Basic Square 8

With eyelets, single color
Color: Orange.

Knit as for Basic Square 1 except for 2 rows with eyelets.
Row 2 (RS): Sl 1 kwise, (k2tog, yo) 5 times, sl 1, k2tog, psso, (yo, k2tog) 5 times, p1.
Row 3 and all wrong side rows: Sl 1 kwise, knit to last st, p1.
Row 4: Sl 1 kwise, knit to the center 3 sts, sl 1, k2tog, psso, knit to last st, p1.
Row 6: Sl 1 kwise, (k2tog, yo), 4 times, sl 1, k2tog, psso, (yo, k2tog) 4 times, p1.
The rest of the square is knitted as for Basic Square 1.

Basic Square 9

"Beaded," 2 colors
Colors: Red-violet and curry.

Knitted as for Basic Square 1 with red-violet and "beads" on Rows 2 and 3.
Row 2 (RS): Curry, preferably a little thicker yarn than the main color or use larger needles. Sl 1 kwise (k1, sl 1 pwise with yarn held behind work on WS) 5 times, sl 1, k2tog, psso, (sl 1 pwise with yarn behind work, k1) 5 times, p1.
Row 3: Curry. Begin with sl 1 kwise, end with p1 and between these sts, knit the curry sts and slip the red-violet sts with yarn behind work (= WS of work).

In Summary

**SQUARE BASICS
END STITCH (END ST)**

◆ K-CO as many or as few sts as you desire, but always use an **uneven number of stitches.**
◆ Knit the pattern you want (Basic Squares 1–9).
◆ **Always** work double decrease over the 3 center sts (sl 1, k2tog, psso) on **all right side rows** (= every other row).
◆ Always slip the first st knitwise and purl the last st (= edge sts).

POTHOLDER 1

*K*nitted with only one square and edged
with a knitted picot border on the bottom.

Measurements: 7.5" × 7.5" (19 × 19 cm)
without the border, 8" × 8" (20 ×
20 cm) with border.
Yarn: *DK weight cotton yarn.*
Colors: Rose, fuchsia and violet.
Needles: Dn 4 (3.5 mm). Circular needle
4 (3.5 mm) for the border.

Technique: Basic Square 1, page 2.
Number of stitches: 75.
Border: "Mouse Teeth"–Knitted Picot.

Instructions

K-CO 75 sts on dn and knit a square with
9 rose ridges, 1 fuchsia, 1 rose, 10 fuchsia,
1 violet, 1 fuchsia ridge and the rest with
violet. When 3 sts remain, knit a 2⅜"–2¾"
(6–7 cm) long strip for the hanging loop.
Turn the loop to the wrong side and sew it
down neatly.

EDGE STITCHES (EDGE STS)

Always knit all first sts on all first
rows. On every subsequent row, the
first st is slipped knitwise (sl 1 kwise,
see Abbreviations, p. 87). The last st
on every row is always purled. It is
easy to pick up and knit sts into this
looped edging and it works well when
you need to cast on at the beginning or
end of a row. Therefore, this edge st is
"required" in domino knitting. When
you pick up and knit sts, insert the
needle under both loops of the edge st.

COLORS

The colors are listed before the instructions. When, for example, it says:
Colors: Rose and tomato, it means

that you first knit with rose and then
with tomato.

ABBREVIATIONS

Go to page 87 to look up any
abbreviations you are not familiar
with. For example, end st, K-CO, sl 1
kwise.

PICKING UP AND KNITTING STITCHES

Always pick up and knit sts with
right side of work facing.
Always place the picked up and
knitted sts so that they are on the needle as knit sts.
Always pick up sts through both
loops of the edge sts.

see instructions in the section on the basic squares, page 3).

Measurements: 7⅛" × 7⅛" (18 × 18 cm) without border; 8⅛" × 8⅛" (20.5 × 20.5 cm) with border.
Yarn: *DK weight cotton yarn.*
Colors: Fuchsia, tomato, rust, rose, old rose.
Needles: Dn 4 (3.5 mm).
Technique: Basic Square 2, page 3.
Number of stitches: 25.
Construction: Vertical panels.
Border: Log Cabin.

Border—Knitted "Mouse Teeth" Picot

With circular ndl, rose, and right side facing, pick up and knit 75–76 sts in the sts of the CO row. Knit 1 row.
Next row: *Using the first st on the needle as the beg st, K-CO 2 new sts, BO 4 sts, move the sts on the right ndl to the left ndl*; repeat *-*. Cut yarn and pull tail through last stitch.

POTHOLDER 2

N ine squares are knitted together in vertical panels worked from the bottom to the top of each strip and then finished with a log cabin border. The potholder is made with garter stitch striped squares (Basic Square 2–

Instructions:

A—1st square—1st panel
Colors: Rose and tomato.

9

NOTE: The first color (rose) listed is the one to use first. K-CO and knit the first row with rose and knit a Basic Square 2. Weave in ends while knitting and finish the square with end st-2, page 3.

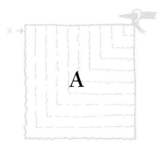

B—2nd square—1st panel
Colors: Fuchsia and tomato.

Place square A as shown in the drawing below. Use end st on A as the first st and then pick up and knit 11 sts along the top of A with fuchsia, going in the direction the needle points (insert ndl through both loops of each st). Go "around the corner," at the little "knot" and pick up and knit 1 st in the CO row st nearest the knot (x on the drawing above); turn work

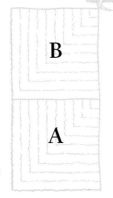

and K-CO 12 new sts (= 25 sts). Knit a square. End st-2.

C—3rd square—1st panel
Colors: Rust and rose.

Knitted as for B over B. End st-3.

1st   0   2nd
panel   panel

D—1st square—2nd panel
Colors: Fuchsia and old rose.

K-CO 12 sts with fuchsia, then, holding the ndl with the sts in the right hand, go "around the corner" at the little knot and pick up and knit 1 st in the nearest CO row st in the lower right corner on A (O on the drawing), and pick up and knit 12 sts along the right side of A (= 25 sts). Knit a square.

E—2nd square—2nd panel
Colors: Old rose and tomato.

Use end st on D and pick up and knit

11 sts over D (= 12 sts total) with old rose, knit 1 st in the top righthand corner of A, where A was finished, and pick up and knit 12 sts along the right side of B (= 25 sts). Knit a square.

F—3rd square—2nd panel
Colors: Fuchsia and tomato.

Knitted as for E over E. When the sts are picked up and knitted, the final st is the end st. End st-3.

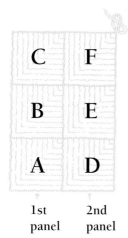

1st   2nd
panel panel

G, H, I—1st, 2nd, and 3rd squares—3rd panel
Colors:
1st square: Tomato and old rose.
2nd square: Rust and fuchsia.
3rd square: Rose and tomato. End st-4.

Knitted as for 1st, 2nd, 3rd squares in

the 2nd panel. Now you have 9 squares joined together.

1st   2nd   3rd
panel panel panel

Log Cabin Border
Color: Rose.

Knit along one side at a time without cutting yarn.

1st side: Begin where square I was finished and pick up and knit about 37 sts along I, F, and C. Knit 3 rows and BO, but leave the last st on the ndl and do not cut yarn.

2nd side: Pick up and knit sts along the edge and then along C, B, and A until you have about 40 sts on the ndl. Knit as for the first side.

3rd side: Same as the 2nd side except along the edges of A, D, and G.

4th side: Pick up and knit sts along the

11

edges of G, H, and I, continuing along the short edge of the 1st side until you have about 43 sts. Knit 3 rows and BO all but the last 3 sts.

Loop: Knit a strip in garter st about 2¾" (7 cm) for the hanging loop. Turn it to the wrong side and sew it down securely.

POTHOLDER 3

16 *small, single color squares are knitted together outwards from the center and then edged all-around with I-cord. The potholder is made of 4 identical blocks of 4 squares each.*

Measurements: 7⅛" × 7⅛" (18 × 18 cm) without border; 7¾" × 7¾" (19.5 × 19.5 cm) with border.

Yarn: *DK weight cotton yarn.*
Colors: Curry, sun yellow, rose, tomato and old rose.
Needles: Dn 4 (3.5 mm); 2 dpn 6 (4 mm) for the border.
Technique: Basic Square 1, page 2.
Number of stitches: 19.
Construction: Outwards from the center.
Border: I-cord.

Instructions

A, B, C, and D—1st block

Knit together 4 single color squares, A (rose), B (curry), C (sun yellow), and D (tomato), as A, B, D, and E on Potholder 2. Square D ends with end st-4. *NOTE:* The center of the potholder is marked on the drawing with a circle.

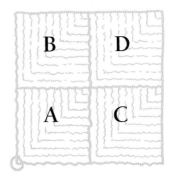

E, F, G, and H—2nd block

Turn the work as shown in the drawing above and knit squares E (curry) and F (old rose) as C and D were knitted onto A and B. Knit G (sun yellow) and H (tomato) onto E and F in the same way.

I, J, K, and L—3rd block

Turn the work again and knit 4 squares, I (tomato), J (curry), K (sun yellow) and L (rose), in the same way as for the 2nd block.

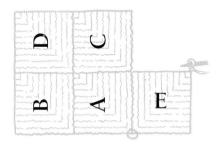

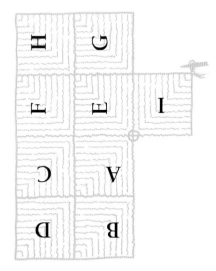

M, N, O, and P—4th block

Turn the work again and knit M (sun yellow) between A and I. Knit N (rose) between M and K. Knit O (old rose) between B and M, and P (curry) between O and N.

NOTE: Note the fine star-patterned structure this potholder has.

I-Cord Border

Color: Tomato.

I-cord makes a rolled edge and is knitted directly onto the piece with 2 dpn. Insert the point of the ndl into a loop at the corner where the edging will begin. Use this loop as the beg-st and K-CO 4 sts (it can be 3–5 sts, but not too many) with tomato.

K3, P2tog (1 tomato and the loop from the potholder). *With yarn held behind the work, insert the point of the ndl through the next pair of edge st loops, from WS to RS. With the ndl in knitting position again, pull the yarn hard behind the work and K3, P2tog (1 tomato and the doubled curry-loops from the potholder)*.

Repeat from *-* around. As the work progresses, tighten the I-cord band so that it lies neatly against the potholder. At the corners, knit 3–5

rows without fastening them to the potholder edge.

Loop: Finish with 2¾"–3⅛" (7–8 cm) I-cord which is not joined to the potholder sts, then, with mattress st, sew the sts together with the I-cord CO. Join the edges of the loop together with a couple of stitches.

POTHOLDER 4

*F*ive squares and four triangles are knitted together in diagonal panels for an octagon. The border is knitted around in garter stitch. The potholder has striped garter stitch squares worked as for Basic Square 2 (see instructions in the section on the basic squares, page 2, and triangles, page 19).

Measurements: 8" × 8" (20 × 20 cm) without border; 8¼" × 8¼" (22.5 × 22.5 cm) with border.

Yarn: *DK weight cotton yarn.*

Colors: Curry, sun yellow, orange, rose, and old rose.

Needles: Dn 4 (3.5 mm). 16" (40 cm) circular needle 4 (3.5 mm) for the border.

Technique: Basic Square 2, page 3.

Number of stitches: 29.

Right- and left-leaning triangles: 15 sts.

Open top and bottom triangles: 29 sts.

Construction: Diagonal panels.

Border: Garter stitch knitted in the round.

Instructions

A—1st panel, a square

Colors: Curry and orange.

   NOTE: The color listed first (curry) is that which is used first. Knit a Basic Square 2.

B—1st panel, a left-leaning triangle

Color: Curry.

Left-leaning triangle

Garter stitch, joined along one side.

Number of stitches: 15, suitable for a square of 29 sts.

1st
panel

Position square A so that the end st is at the top right corner. Use the end st as the first st, then pick up and knit 13 sts along the top left side of A (1 st in each edge st); go "around the corner" at the little "knot" in the corner and pick up and knit 1 st in the nearest CO row st (x on the drawing on previous page) (= 15 sts).

Row 1 (WS): Sl 1 kwise, knit to last st, P1.
Row 2: Sl 1 kwise, knit until 3 sts remain, sl 1, k1, psso, P1.

Repeat these two rows until 3 sts remain.

Next row (WS): Sl 1 kwise, k1, p1.
Next row: Sl 1 kwise, p2tog.
Next row: Sl 1 kwise, p1.
Next row: Sl 1, k1, psso. End st-3.

C—2nd panel, a square

Colors: Old rose and sun yellow.
Knit a separate square.

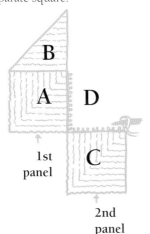

D—2nd panel, a square

Colors: Sun yellow and curry.

Use end st from C, then pick up and knit 13 sts along the top left side of C, go "around the corner" on C and insert the ndl into both the nearest CO st and in the corresponding CO st "around the corner" on A (see arrow on the photo below), pick up and knit 1 st through these loops. Then pick up and knit 14 sts along the top right side of A (= 29) sts. Knit a square.

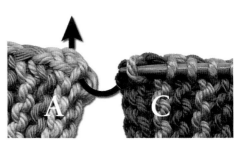

E—2nd panel, a square

Colors: Rose and sun yellow.

Use end st from D, then pick up and knit 13 sts along the top left side of D. Pick up and knit 1 st in the top corner of A and 14 sts along the top right side of B. Knit a square.

F—3rd panel, a right-leaning triangle
Color: Orange.

Right-leaning triangle
Garter stitch, joined along one side.
   F is a triangle on the right side of the work, knitted next to square C.
Number of stitches: 15, suitable for squares of 29 sts.

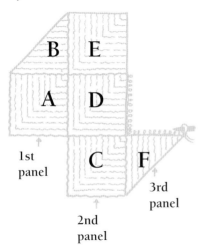

1st panel

2nd panel

3rd panel

Go "around the corner" on C and pick up and knit 1 st in the CO st nearest the knot, then pick up and knit 14 sts along the top right side of C (= 15 sts).
Row 1 (WS): Sl 1 kwise, knit to last st, p1.
Row 2 (RS): Sl 1 kwise, K2tog, knit to last st, p1.
Repeat these 2 rows decreasing on every RS row until 3 sts remain.

Next row (WS): Sl 1 kwise, k1, p1.
Next row: Sl 1 kwise, p2tog.
Next row: Sl 1 kwise, p1.
Next row: Sl 1, k1, psso.

G—3rd panel, a square
Colors: Rose and curry.
   Pick up and knit a total of 29 sts in the notch between F and D with the center st in the corner of C and knit a square.

H—3rd panel, a top triangle
Colors: Sun yellow.

Top triangle, open—29 sts
   Joined along 2 sides. The triangle ends with sts on the ndl which you can use to continue knitting. These triangles can be worked upwards or downwards.

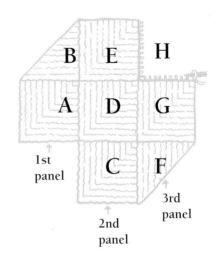

1st panel

2nd panel

3rd panel

17

Number of stitches: 29.

Use the end st from G, then pick up and knit 13 sts along the top left side of G, pick up and knit 1 st on the corner of D and 13 sts along the top right side of E, and, finally, use the end st of E (= 29 sts).

Row 1 (WS): Knit to the last st, p1.

Row 2 (RS): Sl 1 kwise, k12, sl 1, k2tog, psso, k11, p1, turn work, leaving last st on ndl.

Row 3: Sl 1 kwise, k23, p1, turn work, leaving last st on ndl.

Row 4: Sl 1 kwise, k10, sl 1, k2tog, psso, k9, p1, turn work.

Row 5: Sl 1 kwise, k19, p1, turn work.

Row 6: Sl 1 kwise, k8, sl 1, k2tog, psso, k7, p1, turn work.

Row 7: Sl 1 kwise, k15, p1, turn work.

Row 8: Sl 1 kwise, k6, sl 1, k2tog, psso, k5, p1, turn work.

Row 9: Sl 1 kwise, k11, p1, turn work.

Row 10: Sl 1 kwise, k4, sl 1, k2tog, psso, k3, p1, turn work.

Row 11: Sl 1 kwise, k7, p1, turn work.

Row 12: Sl 1 kwise, k2, sl 1, k2tog, psso, k1, p1, turn work.

Row 13: Sl 1 kwise, k3, p1, turn.

Row 14: Sl 1 kwise, sl 1, k2tog, psso (= 15 sts).

Place all sts on a stitch holder or piece of yarn.

I—a bottom triangle

Color: Sun yellow.

Turn the work upside down and knit a bottom triangle (= top triangle) in the notch between squares C and A.

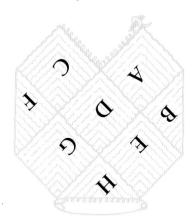

Bottom triangle, open—29 sts

A bottom triangle is knitted in the same way as the top triangle above but there is no end st to begin or end with. Here, you pick up and knit sts from the CO row.

Border—Garter st in the round

With circular ndl and sun yellow, pick up and knit about 14 sts closely spaced along the outer edge of each square/triangle (= about 112 sts). Work (1 purl rnd, 1 knit rnd on which you inc 1 st at each of the 8 corners) twice; purl 1 rnd and then BO.

Loop: Pick up and knit 3 sts at the top of the potholder and knit a garter stitch strip 2¾" (7 cm) long. BO; turn the loop to the wrong side and sew it down securely.

Triangles

RIGHT-/LEFT-LEANING TRIANGLES WITH VARIOUS NUMBERS OF STITCHES

Use the stitch count from a square. Subtract 1 st (corresponding to the center st) and divide the rest of the sts by 2. Add 1 st. For example: 29 sts-1 st = 28 sts, divided by 2 = 14 sts+1 st = 15 sts.

The result of this mathematical formula is the number of sts you should use for a right- or left-leaning triangle.

OPEN-TOP/BOTTOM TRIANGLES WITH VARIOUS NUMBER OF STITCHES

The principle for top and bottom triangles is the same except for the number of sts you use (uneven number). Be careful that all the sl 1, k2tog, pssos come together over each other and always have 1 st remaining at the end of the ndl at the end of the 2nd and all following rows. Finish top and bottom triangles as evenly as possible.

FINISHED TOP AND BOTTOM TRIANGLES

You can also bind off top and bottom triangles instead of leaving the sts. Work by binding off 1 st at the beginning of the first and all following rows, until all the sts are bound off.

HEADBAND OR TURBAN

*K*nit it wide and use it as is or pull it together with a brooch or a knitted band–or knit it smaller as a headband. The technique involves squares placed diamond-wise in a ring and joined without sewing.

Size: Child (adult).

Measurements: Total circumference is about 17¾" (19¾") (45 [50] cm) (unstretched measurement); it stretches out with use.

Yarn: *Fine wool yarn, 225 m/50 g.*

Colors for child's size: Partial skeins of charcoal gray, white, pink, and orange.

Colors for adult size: Partial skeins of charcoal gray, white, gray, and gold-brown.

Needles: Dn 2 (3 mm). For the rolled edging, use 16" (40 cm) circular ndl 2 (3 mm).

Technique: Basic Square 2, page 3.

Number of stitches: 25.

Open top/bottom triangle: 25 sts.

Construction: In a ring with the squares set diamond-wise.

Gauge: A square should measure 1¼" (4.7 cm) in width and height and 2⅝" (6.7 cm) diagonally from corner to corner.

Border: Rolled edge in purl stitch.

Instructions

The headband is knitted in striped squares which are knitted together in a ring over each other.

Round 1
Colors: White and charcoal gray (gray, charcoal gray).

Knit 6 (7) separate but identical squares.

Round 2
Colors: Charcoal gray and white (charcoal gray, white).

Place all 6 (7) squares in a row with the corners "hand in hand," so that all the end sts point upwards and the corners with the CO rows are at the bottom.

Between two squares there is a notch and this is where you will knit in the new square. See Potholder 4, where square D is knitted between A and C. Knit a total of 5 (6) squares, one in each notch.

Arrange the piece into a ring where the first and the last squares are "hand in hand" and knit a sixth (seventh) square in the notch which remains. Now you have a ring consisting of 2 rounds with 6 (7) squares in each round.

Round 3
Colors: Gray, charcoal gray.

For the child's size, the headband should be narrow so don't knit Round 3. For the adult size: Knit a square in each notch.

Round 4
Color: Pink (gold-brown).

Knit an open top triangle with 25 sts in each notch.

Row 1 (WS): K24, p1.
Row 2 (RS): Sl 1 kwise, k10, sl 1, k2tog, psso, k9, p1, turn work, leaving last st on ndl.
Row 3: Sl 1 kwise, k19, p1, turn work, leaving last st on ndl.
Row 4: Sl 1 kwise, k8, sl 1, k1, psso, k7, p1, turn.
Row 5: Sl 1 kwise, k15, p1, turn.
Row 6: Sl 1 kwise, k6, sl 1 k2tog, psso, k5, p1, turn.

A B C D E F *Round 1*

Hand in Hand

Round 2

Row 7: Sl 1 kwise, k11, p1, turn.

Row 8: Sl 1 kwise, k4, sl 1, k2tog, psso, k3, p1, turn.

Row 9: Sl 1 kwise, k7, p1, turn.

Row 10: Sl 1 kwise, k2, sl 1, k2tog, psso, k1, p1, turn.

Row 11: Sl 1 kwise, k3, p1, turn.

Row 12: Sl 1 kwise, sl 1, k2tog, psso (= 13 sts).

Border: Place all remaining sts on a circular ndl (13 sts per triangle) and purl 5 rnds, picking up and knitting 1 st between each triangle on the first rnd. BO loosely in purl.

Turn the work upside down and knit bottom triangles with orange (gold-brown) in the notches on the other side, and finish with a border in the same way as for the top.

Joining Squares in Pyramids

When knitting both in the round and in diagonal panels, it seems logical to knit squares together in pyramids. There are no references to pyramids in the instructions, but you can join squares in that fashion when it seems logical. Here you can see how it is done: Knit 2 separate squares A and B.

Do not cut ends. Place the squares next to each other diamondwise and meeting "hand in hand," Knit square C in the notch between A and B. Knit a separate square D, and then a new square E in the notch between D and B. Continue with square F between E and C. Now you can see a little pyramid.

In Summary

JOINING SQUARES
Squares can be knitted together in panels, rounds, and/or pyramids.

PANELS
When squares are knitted together in panels, always work up starting at the bottom and always from left to right.

ROUNDS
When the squares are joined in rounds, knit the new squares in the notches between squares "standing" on their corners diamond-wise. It doesn't matter whether you work to the right or left.

PYRAMIDS
A combination of both techniques.

STRIPS— POTHOLDER 5— JOINING 1

5 striped strips with 2 rows of knit sts between each strip and a ribbed border– no magic needed!

Measurements: 6¾" × 6¾" (17 × 17 cm) without border, 8¼" × 8¼" (21 × 21 cm) with border.

Yarn: *DK weight cotton yarn.*

Colors: Yellow-green, green, and curry.

Needles: Dpn 4 (3.5 mm); 16" (40 cm) circular ndl 4 (3.5 mm) for the border.

Technique: Strips. Joining 1.

Pattern: Striped Garter Stitch (= checker-board).

Border: Ribbing worked in the round.

Tip: *Weave in as many ends as possible while knitting.*

Instructions

1st Strip

Colors: Yellow-green, green, curry.

With yellow-green and dpn, K-CO 7 sts.

Row 1 (RS): Knit to the last st, end p1.

Row 2 (WS): Sl 1 kwise, knit to last st, end p1.

NOTE: The yarn end hangs on the left side when you are on RS rows.

Repeat the second row until you have knitted a total of 6 ridges on RS; then knit 1 ridge (= 2 rows) with green, 6 curry ridges, 1 green, 6 yellow-green, 1 green, 6 curry, 1 green, and, finally, 5 ridges and 1 row on RS with yellow-green. Now there should be 33 ridges on RS and 34 on WS.

BO on WS; cut yarn and pull end through last st (end st), but do not pull the thread tight (= end st-3).

When you bind off, there are 34 ridges on both right and wrong sides and 34 edge sts.

NOTE: End st is at the top right.

Joining 1

1st joining stripe—a garter st ridge
Color: Green.

This joining stripe is a vertical ridge of garter st on the right side of the 1st strip.

Use a dpn or circular ndl and green yarn.

Beginning at the bottom, go "around the corner" on the right side of the knot and pick up and knit 1 sts on RS in the nearest CO st.

Then pick up and knit 34 sts, 1 in each edge st, inserting ndl under both loops of each edge st along the 1st strip and ending with 1 in the loose end st (= 36 sts). Pull the thread through the end st.

Now you have 2 sts more than there are ridges and edge sts. These 2 extra sts will be eliminated later.

Turn the work and knit back, sl 1 kwise, knit until

2 sts remain, **p2tog** (= 35 sts).

Now one of the extra sts has been eliminated and there is only one extra st left. It will be eliminated on the 2nd strip.

Cut yarn.

2nd strip
Colors: Curry, green, yellow-green.

Knit a new garter stitch strip together with stitches from the first joining stripe (JS). Use the lowest JSst (joining stripe stitch) as the beg st and K-CO 7 new sts with curry extending out from JS.

Row 1 (RS): K6, p2tog (1 st from the strip and 1 JSst). Turn work.

Row 2: Sl 1 kwise, knit to last st, p1.

Row 3: Sl 1 kwise, k5, p2tog (1 st from strip and 1 JSst). Turn work.

Repeat Rows 2 and 3 in stripes as for the first

strip, but in this color order: *6 curry ridges, 1 green, 6 yellow-green, 1 green*. Repeat *-* until 2 green JSsts remain. Knit one row on WS.

Next row (RS): Sl 1 kwise, k5, **p3tog** (1 green and 2 yellow-green sts).

Now the last of the 2 extra sts has been eliminated.

BO on wrong side. Leave the end st loose. Now there are 34 ridges on both

right and wrong sides. Weave in all ends except the curry end st tail.

2nd joining stripe
As for the 1st joining stripe.

3rd strip
With yellow-green, K-CO 7 sts and knit as for the 2nd strip but with the same color sequence as in strip 1.

3rd joining stripe
As for the first joining stripe.

4th strip
As for the 2nd strip.

4th joining stripe
As for the 1st joining stripe.

5th strip
As for the 3rd strip.

Border—Ribbing worked in the round
With green yarn and circular ndl, pick up and knit about 35 sts evenly spaced along each of the four sides and 1 st in each corner. Purl 1 rnd, knit 1 rnd and then work 3 rnds k1, p1 ribbing. On the first rnd of ribbing, inc 1 st on each side of each corner st. BO in ribbing.

Loop: Pick up and knit 4 sts in one corner; knit a strip about 2¾" (7 cm) long and BO. Sew the loop securely on the wrong side.

25

JOINING STRIPES–NUMBER OF STITCHES

When you pick up stitches for a joining stripe, you can sometimes have a stitch too few or too many. It doesn't matter so much if a joining stripe has one or several rows after the row on which stitches were picked up. Simply adjust the number of stitches on the next row (by increasing or decreasing). If you are not going to knit several rows, you should have the correct number of stitches at the beginning.

COUNTING THREAD

A counting thread is a marking thread which is used to count stitches, rows or ridges. It is recommended that you always have about a yard/meter of colored cotton thread on hand.

In Summary

STRIPS

◆ K-CO as many or as few sts as desired.

◆ Knit the pattern you have chosen with 1 edge st at each side.

◆ Always BO on the wrong side.

POTHOLDER 6— JOINING 2

3 garter stitch and 2 pattern-knitted strips with 1 knit row in between. Surrounding them all is a pretty and useful border.

Measurements: 6¾" × 6¾" (17.5 × 17.5 cm) without border, 8⅛" × 8⅛" (20.5 × 20.5 cm) with border.
Yarn: *DK weight cotton yarn.*
Colors: Turquoise, curry, and mint.
Needles: Dpn 4 (3.5 mm). 16" (40 cm) circular needle 4 (3.5 mm) for the border.
Techniques: Strips. Joining 2.
Patterns: Garter stitch and 2-color knit and purl stripes.
Border: Narrow strip.

Instructions

1st strip

Color: Turquoise.

K-CO 7 sts and knit a strip as for the first strip on Potholder 5, but here there should be 35 ridges on RS before and 36 ridges after binding off.

1st and 3rd joining stripes—a knit row

Color: Curry.

The first joining stripe is a vertical knitted row worked on the right side of the first strip. Using a dpn or circular needle, begin at the lower edge, go "around the corner" on the right side of the knot and pick up and knit 1 st on RS in the nearest

CO st. Then, pick up and knit 36 sts, 1 st in each edge st, through both loops, and finish with k1 in end st (= 38 sts).

Now there are 2 sts more than the number of ridges or edge sts. These extra two sts will be eliminated later. Cut yarn.

2nd strip

Colors: Curry and mint.

Use the lowest st on the joining stripe as the beg st and K-CO 8 new sts with curry extending out from JS.

Row 1 (RS): K7, p2tog (1 st from strip and 1 JSst). Turn work.

Row 2: Sl 1 kwise, knit to last st, p1.

Row 3: Sl 1 kwise, p6, **p3 tog** (1 st from the strip and 1 JSst). Turn work.

Now the first of the 2 extra sts has been eliminated and there is only one extra st.

Row 4: Sl 1 kwise, knit to last st, p1.

Row 5: Mint–Sl 1 kwise, k6, p2 tog. Turn work.

Row 6: Sl 1 kwise, purl to end of row.

Row 7: Curry–Sl 1 kwise, k6, p2 tog. Turn work.

Repeat Rows 2 to 7 for the rest of the strip. Finish on WS when 2 JSsts remain.

Next row (RS): Sl 1 kwise, k6, **p3 tog.**

Now the last of the 2 extra sts has been eliminated. BO on WS. Do not pull the tail through end st. Now there are 36 edge sts on the right side again.

Counting Rows and Ridges

When you need to count rows/ridges on a long strip (garter st in the drawing), it is a good idea to weave in a counting thread after 5 ridges (= 10 rows) and out after the next 5 ridges (= 10 rows), etc.

The counting thread is worked in like a tacking thread with 10 rows in between and makes it easier to see where you are in the work.

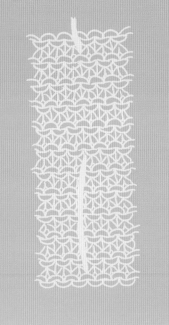

2nd and 4th joining stripes
Color: Turquoise.

Worked as for the first joining stripe.

3rd strip
Color: Turquoise.

K-CO 7 sts extending out from JS.

Row 1 (RS): K6, p2tog (1 st from the strip and 1 JSst). Turn work.

Row 2: Sl 1 kwise, k5, p1.

Row 3: Sl 1 kwise, k5, **p3 tog.** Turn work.

Now the first of the 2 extra sts has been eliminated and there is only 1 extra st left.

Row 4: As for Row 2.

Row 5: Sl 1 kwise, k5, p2tog. Turn work.

Repeat Rows 4 and 5 until 2 sts of the 2nd joining stripe remain. The last row is knitted on the RS.

Next row (WS): Sl 1 kwise, k5, p1.

Next row: Sl 1 kwise, K5, p3 tog.

Now the last extra st has been eliminated.

BO on WS.

Now there are 36 ridges on each side.

4th strip
Worked as for 2nd strip

5th strip
Worked as for 3rd strip.

Border in a narrow strip
With mint and circular ndl, pick up and knit sts evenly divided around, about 35–36 sts along each side and 1 st at each corner.

Purl 1 row. Change to curry. Use the last mint st on the circular ndl as the beg st, K-CO 3 sts in curry extending out from sts on the circular ndl. Use a dpn to help.

Row 1: K2, p2 tog (= 1 curry and 1 mint st). Turn work.

Row 2: K2, p1.

Row 3: Sl 1 kwise, k1, p2tog (1 curry and 1 mint st). Turn work.

Repeat Rows 2 and 3 around until all the mint sts have been knitted away. Do not cut yarn or BO.

Loop: Knit 2¾–3" (7–8 cm) straight up over the 3 curry sts. BO. Turn loop to WS and sew securely with duplicate st.

POTHOLDER 7— JOINING 3

A stockinette knitted strip in two colors, with a new strip knitted directly onto the first. A sweet sawtooth border completes the picture.

Measurements: 6¾" × 6¾" (17 × 17 cm) without border, 8" × 8" (20 × 20 cm) with border.

Yarn: *DK weight cotton yarn.*

Colors: Light blue, mint, light green.

Needles: Dn 4 (3.5 mm). 16" (40 cm) circular ndl 4 (3.5 mm) for the border.

Technique: Strips. Joining 3.

Pattern: Stockinette.

Border: Sawtooth edging.

Instructions

1st strip

Colors: Light blue and mint.

With light blue and dn, K-CO 19 sts.

Row 1 (RS): Knit to last st, p1.

Row 2 (WS): Sl 1 kwise, purl to end of row.

Repeat Rows 1 and 2 a total of 12 times = 24 rows. Change to mint and work another 25 rows.

BO on WS, cut yarn, pull tail through last st (end st), but don't pull it tight (= end st-3). There are now 50 ridges on WS of work. With RS facing, the CO tail hangs on the left bottom corner and the BO tail is in the upper right corner.

Joining 3
2nd strip—without a joining stripe
Colors: Light green and light blue.

There is no joining stripe between the two strips.

Using the last CO st in the CO row at the lower right hand corner of the 1st strip as the beg st, K-CO 19 new sts with light green.

Row 1 (RS): K18, p2tog (the last light green st and the beg st). Turn work.

Row 2 (WS): Sl 1 kwise, purl to end of row. Turn work, insert the end of the needle closest to the 1st strip into the second edge st—**skipping first edge st**. The needle is inserted through both loops of the edge st, going from back to front of work—see photo, above. Slide ndl back into position for working next row.

Row 3 (RS): Sl 1 kwise, k17, p2 tog (the next light blue st and the edge st, through both loops. Turn work.

Row 4 (WS): Sl 1 kwise, purl to end of row.

Turn work, insert the end of the needle closest to the 1st strip into the next edge st. Needle is inserted through both loops of edge st, going from back to front of work. Slide ndl back into position for working next row.

Repeat Rows 3 and 4 until 1 light blue edge st remains (or 24 rows). Change to light blue and continue until 1 mint edge st remains. Skip over it and, instead, work the last row this way:

Next row: Sl 1 kwise, k17, p2tog (the last st and end st on the 1st strip). Turn work and BO. Cut yarn.

Sawtooth Border

With circular ndl 4 (3.5 mm) and light blue yarn, pick up and knit 24 sts along each of the 4 sides and purl 1 row.

Triangles:

Row 1: With light green—use a dpn to help if necessary. Use the first light blue st as beg st and K-CO 1 light green st. K2. (1 light green and 1 light blue st). Turn work.

Row 2: K1, p1.

Row 3: Sl 1 kwise, k2 (3 light green sts). Turn work.

Row 4: K2, p1.

Row 5: Sl 1 kwise, k3 (4 light green sts). Turn work.

Row 6: K3, p1.

Row 7: Sl 1 kwise, k4 (5 light green sts). Turn work.

Row 8: K4, p1.

Row 9: BO 4 sts loosely * and knit 1 more light blue st. Turn work.

Repeat Rows 2–9 up to the *; now you have 3 light green triangles. Change to mint and knit 1 light blue st. Turn work and repeat Rows 2–9 again. Now there are 3 mint triangles and 6 triangles total along one side. Continue in the same manner on the next side, knitting 6 triangles. Repeat these 2 sides on the following 2 sides.

Loop: With mint, on back of work pick up and knit 4 sts and knit a strip about 2¾" (7 cm) long. Sew down loop securely with duplicate st.

Joining 3 in Garter Stitch

Garter stitch pieces can be knitted together in the same way.

NOTE: In this joining, the ridges on RS meet like fingers in clasped hands.

BINDING OFF ON STRIPS
Strips are always bound off on WS. Finish with end st-3.

STRIPS IN PATTERNS OTHER THAN GARTER STITCH
You can knit strips in garter stitch, but also in many other patterns such as stockinette, cables, moss st, etc. When you are knitting ridges (garter st) together, it is easiest to count the ridges in order to determine how many sts are needed on the next joining stripe. In stockinette and other patterns, you can count edge sts.

POTHOLDER 8

*G*arter stitch strips and cables with 2 knit rows in between. The border is worked in reverse stockinette. The potholder is knitted as for Potholder 5, but the 2nd and 4th strips have cable patterns.

Measurements: 6¾" × 6¾" (17 × 17 cm) without border, 7¾" × 7¾" (19.5 × 19.5 cm) with border.

Yarn: *DK weight cotton yarn.*

Colors: Mint, dark blue, and blue.

Needles: Dpn 4 (3.5 mm). Cable ndl. 16" (40 cm) circular ndl 4 (3.5 mm) for border.

Technique: Strips. Joining 1.

Patterns: Garter st. Cables following chart. Chart is repeated throughout.

Border: Purl stitch rolled edging.

Instructions

1st strip
Color: Mint. As for Potholder 5, but in one color.

1st, 2nd, 3rd, and 4th in-between stripes.
Color: Dark blue. As for Potholder 5.

2nd and 4th strips—cables
Color: Blue.

Use the lowest JSst as the beg st and K-CO 9 new sts.

Row 1 (RS): K8, p2tog (1 st from strip and 1 JSst); turn.

Rows 2 and 4: Sl 1 kwise, purl to end of row.

☐   Stockinette = Knit on RS and purl on WS.

Place 3 sts on a cable ndl behind work, k3, knit sts from cable ndl.

Place 3 sts on cable ndl in front of work, k3, knit sts from cable ndl.

What is a Ridge?

There are two types of ridges:

**GARTER STITCH RIDGES AND
   PURL RIDGES**
1 garter stitch ridge = 2 knitted rows.
   These two rows make one ridge and
   in the instructions are simply called
   a ridge.
1 purl ridge = actually a knit row seen
   from the wrong side where the purl
   ridge is obvious or a purl row
   worked on the right side where it
   looks like a purl ridge. A purl st

ridge is called a purl ridge in the
instructions.
   It is these ridges which are count-
ed. In garter stitch, there are ridges on
both right and wrong sides. In stockinette, there are ridges only on the
wrong (purl) side.

Row 3: Sl 1 kwise, inc 2 sts (inc with M1b)
   evenly spaced over the next 7 sts
   (which are knitted), p2 tog (= 11 sts);
   turn.
Row 5: Sl 1 kwise, the next 9 sts are the 1st
   row on the chart (begin at arrow), p2
   tog; turn.

Continue working the pattern, following the chart for the 9 center sts, knit the
strip's last st tog with JSst and work 1 edge
st on the free side. When 2 JSsts remain,

BO 2 sts on RS. BO on WS.
3rd and 5th strips.
Color: Mint. As for Potholder 5.

Purl Stitch Rolled Edging

   With circular ndl and dark blue, pick
up and knit sts around the whole potbold-
er (with the same number of sts on each
side), K-CO 8 sts on one corner for the
loop and purl 4 rows. BO purlwise. Turn
the edging to WS and sew down.

In Summary
Joining Strips

◆ Knit a strip.

◆ Count the number of edge stitches.

JOINING 1
—*with 1 garter st ridge as a joining stripe*

◆ Pick up and knit sts along the right side of the strip (1 st for each RS ridge/edge st + 2 sts), picking up the first st in the nearest K-CO st "around the corner" and the last st in the end st.

◆ Knit back as follows: Sl 1 kwise, knit until 2 sts remain, p2 tog.

◆ K-CO new sts extending out from the joining stripe sts.

◆ Knit a new strip which is knitted onto the previous strip, but finish with p3 tog when 2 joining stripe sts remain.

◆ BO on wrong side.

JOINING 2
—*with 1 knit row as a joining stripe*

◆ Pick up and knit sts along the right side of the strip (1 st for each RS ridge/edge st + 2 sts), picking up the first st in the nearest K-CO st "around the corner" and the last st in the end st.

◆ K-CO new sts extending out from the joining stripe sts.

◆ Knit a new strip which is knitted onto the previous strip, but the 2nd row (RS) and all last rows on the right side are finished with p3 tog.

◆ BO on wrong side.

JOINING 3
—*without a joining stripe*

◆ Begin "around the corner" and use the nearest stitch in the cast-on row as beg st where you will then cast on sts for the new strip.

◆ Knit the new strip onto the previous one, with 2 rows of the new strip for each edge st in the old but skip over the first and last edge sts and knit the last st in end st.

Domino Projects
You can Knit

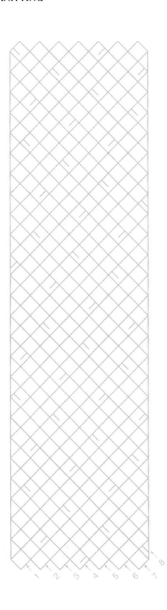

SHAWL, THROW, OR SCARF

*H*ere are the instructions for a long and lovely shawl. Make it narrower and shorter for a scarf or longer and wider for a throw.

Design: Kirsten Jensen

Width: 23⅝" (60 cm).
Length: 87" (220 cm) plus tassels.
Yarn: *Sport weight wool yarn.*
Colors: 550 g unbleached white and small amounts of yarns in shades you desire for the shawl. Here we've used rust, beige, yellow-green, curry, pale yellow, and light green. You'll need less yarn for a scarf and more for a throw.
Needles: Dn 2 (3 mm).
Technique: Basic Square 1, p. 2, plus a variation of this, see below.
Number of stitches: 29.
Right- and left-leaning triangles: p. 19, 15 sts.
Construction: Diagonal panels, as for Potholder 4, p. 15.
Gauge: A square should measure 2⅜" (6 cm) in width and height and 3½" (8.5 cm) diagonally from corner to corner.
Gauge swatch: Knit panels 1, 2, and 3 following the chart and measure the gauge on the center square.

Instructions

The whole shawl is knitted with unbleached white. Knit the squares following the diagram. The diagram shows the entire shawl. Begin with the first panel, then the 2nd panel, etc., as for panels A–E on Potholder 4.

3rd panel, 3rd square is a square with ½ stockinette ridge on the right side, see diagram. The square is knitted as for Basic Square 1, but Row 3 (WS) is knitted as follows: Sl 1 kwise, k13, purl to end of row.

5th panel, 8th square is a square with ½ stockinette ridge on the left side, see diagram. The square is knitted as for Basic Square 1, but Row 3 (WS) is worked as follows: Sl 1 kwise, p12, knit to last st, p1.

Finishing

When you have finished knitting the shawl, use duplicate st to embroider 1–2 rows with 12 colored duplicate sts centered on each and every of the stockinette rows on the squares which are marked with diagonal right- and left-leaning streaks on the diagram. Divide the colors evenly over the entire shawl. Make tassels and sew them firmly on the corner of each square along both of the shawl's short ends.

SQUARE PILLOW

*A*s easy as it comes. Knit squares from the center outwards, turn the work to the wrong side and sew together.

Measurements: 14½" × 14½" (37 × 37 cm).
Yarn: *Fingering weight wool yarn.* Silke Tweed from Garnstudio.
Colors: 65 g granite, 65 g unbleached white.
Needles: Dn 2 (3 mm).
 You will also need a pillow form at least 2" (5 cm) larger than the pillow's measurements.
Technique: Basic Square 5, p. 5.
Number of stitches: 25.
Construction: From the center and outwards, as for Potholder 3, p. 12.
Gauge: One square should measure about 2" (5 cm) in width and height and 3" (7.5 cm) diagonally from corner to corner.

Instructions

 The pillow is knitted following the same principles as for Potholder 3, but each block has 9 panels with 9 squares in each row (= 81 squares). On the 1st and 3rd quarters (diagonally over each other), you cast on and knit the garter ridges with granite and the stockinette rows

with unbleached white. On the 2nd and 4th quarters, reverse the color sequence.

Finishing

 Carefully press the work. Turn the corners in towards each other on the wrong side of the pillow and sew them together with mattress stitch on the right side, starting at the corners and out to all 4 sides. However, leave an opening for the pillow form. After inserting the form, sew the opening together. Then sew a button on through all layers.

RECTANGULAR PILLOW

*T*he cable-patterned section in the center is knitted first and then the patterns to the right are worked with garter ridges in between. Turn the work and knit a matching section on the other side. The I-cord border has knots at each corner.

Measurements: 12⅞" × 16½" (32 × 42 cm)
Yarn: *Fingering weight wool yarn.* Silke Tweed from Garnstudio.
Colors: 1¾ oz (50 g) unbleached white, 1 oz (25 g) granite, ½ oz (15 g) beige.
Needles: Dn and 24" (60 cm) circular ndl 2 (3 mm) and a cable ndl. 2 dpn 4 (3.5 mm) for the border.

You will also need a pillow form at least 2" (5 cm) larger than the pillow cover and a piece of fabric large enough to cover the back of the pillow + seam allowance.

Technique: Strips. Joining 1, as for Potholder 5, p. 23.

Patterns: All the patterns are knitted following the charts. Begin on RS at the arrow. The section within heavy dark lines is the pattern repeat which is repeated, working upwards for length of strip.

Border: I-cord, see Potholder 3, p. 12.

Instructions

1st strip—center
Color: Unbleached white.

K-CO 41 sts and work 12½" (32 cm) with Pattern 1 with 1 edge st at each side. BO. Continue, working to the right, alternating a joining stripe and a strip.

A joining stripe
Color: Unbleached white.

See Potholder 5 and knit as for the 1st joining stripe.

BEGINNING STITCH (BEG ST)

A beginning st is needed when you begin a knit cast-on. Place a slip knot onto the needle and begin K-CO from there.

When you want to join a square or a strip to another you can, for example, use the nearest CO st "around the corner" as the beg st.

In principle, you can insert the needle into a stitch loop where you wish in the work and use it as a beg st when you cast on.

ARE THE EDGE STITCHES TOO LOOSE?

It is important that the edge sts not be too loose. It is a problem which is easy to correct. When you knit the stitch after the edge stitch you can pull a little on the thread with the left index finger while you knit and thereby pull the edge stitch, so that it becomes as even and fine as the rest of the stitches in the work. This little pulling quickly becomes a habit which you won't even think about.

I-CORD ON TWO NEEDLES

K-CO with dpn, for example, 5 sts. Turn the work and slide the sts to the other end of ndl, with yarn behind work to the right and pull it. Knit 5 sts, slide sts to other end of ndl, with yarn behind and knit another row. Continue in this way and pull at the yarn afterwards.

Pattern 1

Pattern 2

Pattern 3

Pattern 4

Pattern 5

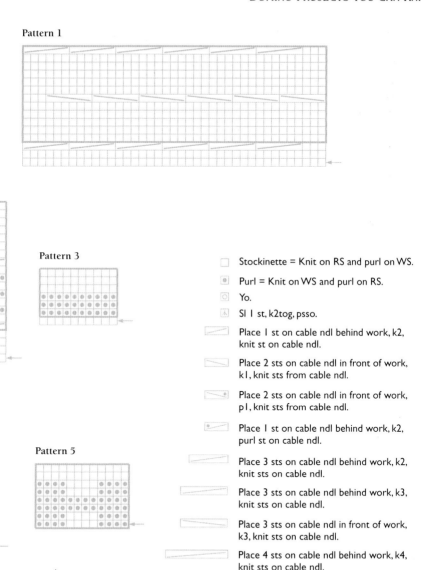

Stockinette = Knit on RS and purl on WS.

Purl = Knit on WS and purl on RS.

Yo.

Sl 1 st, k2tog, psso.

Place 1 st on cable ndl behind work, k2, knit st on cable ndl.

Place 2 sts on cable ndl in front of work, k1, knit sts from cable ndl.

Place 2 sts on cable ndl in front of work, p1, knit sts from cable ndl.

Place 1 st on cable ndl behind work, k2, purl st on cable ndl.

Place 3 sts on cable ndl behind work, k2, knit sts on cable ndl.

Place 3 sts on cable ndl behind work, k3, knit sts on cable ndl.

Place 3 sts on cable ndl in front of work, k3, knit sts on cable ndl.

Place 4 sts on cable ndl behind work, k4, knit sts on cable ndl.

2nd strip

Color: Granite. 10 sts.

Knit this strip onto the joining stripe. K-CO 10 sts extending out from the JS (at the first strip's cast-on). Knit Pattern 2 with 1 edge st at each side, one of which will be used for the joining. Finish with K3tog when 2 JSsts remain. Join the following strips with edge sts in the same way.

3rd strip

Color: Beige.

K-CO 12 sts and work Pattern 3.

4th strip

Color: Unbleached white.

K-CO 9 sts and work Pattern 4.

5th strip

Color: Granite.

K-CO 14 sts and work Pattern 5. You have now finished the right side. Turn the work and work the other side in the same way. Using a steam iron, steam the piece, shaping it so that edges are straight but do not press down on the knitting or the patterns will flatten out.

Border—I-cord with knots

Knit an I-cord border (See Potholder 3) along all 4 sides, but, in each corner, knit a 2⅜"–2¾" (6–7 cm) long piece without connecting it to the pillow. Place the sts on a safety pin (do not cut yarn) and make a knot in the cord. Sew the border (ends of the cord) together with duplicate st.

Finishing

Sew the fabric backing to the cover but leave an opening for the pillow cushion. Insert cushion and sew the opening together.

TABLE MAT

*V*ery simple table mat in white linen.

Measurements: 11¾" × 16½" (30 × 42 cm).
Yarn: *Heavy linen yarn.* Medium weight cotton yarn will also work.
Color: 85 g unbleached white.
Needles: Dn 2 (3 mm).
Technique: Basic Square 8, p. 7.

Number of stitches: 25.
Right- and left-leaning triangles: P. 19, 13 sts.
Construction: Diagonal panels, as for Potholder 4, p. 15.
Gauge: A square should measure 2" (5 cm) in width and height and 3" (7.5 cm) diagonally from corner to corner.

Instructions

Follow the diagram, using the same principles as Potholder 4. The numbers show the order in which the panels should be knitted; the letters indicate the order of the squares in a panel. The first block in the 5th panel is a right-leaning triangle.

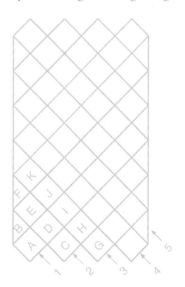

COFFEEPOT COVER

Your coffeepot might need a "coat" to keep it warm. This coffeepot cover is both fun to knit and nice to look at and fits a common coffeepot.

Height: 11¾" (30 cm).
Circumference: 19⅝" (50 cm).
Yarn: *Fine linen yarn.*
Colors: 3½ oz (100 g) white and 3½ oz (100 g) black.
Needles: Dn 1 (2.5 mm).
You will also need 2 buttons and a piece of 13¾" × 23⅝" (35 × 60 cm) lining fabric.
Technique: Basic Squares 1 and 2, p. 2.
Number of stitches: 27.
Open top triangle: 27 sts.
Striped squares and triangles: Pick up and knit sts and work Row 1 with black, and then alternately work 2 rows white and 2 rows black.
Right- and left-leaning triangles: p. 19, 14 sts.
Construction: From the center and outwards, as for Potholders 2 and 3, and standing on their corners diamondwise, as for Headband, p 19.
Gauge: A square should measure 2⅛" (5.5 cm) in width and height and 3⅛" (8 cm) diagonally from corner to corner.
Diagram: Knit the squares and triangles in the order indicated by the numbers and with the colors which are listed next to the diagram.

Instructions

See diagram and knit squares 1, 2, 3, and 4 together, as for Potholder 2 (A, B, D, E), in straight rows, starting at the bottom. Then knit squares 5, 6, 7, and 8 together in straight rows, from the center outwards, as for Potholder 3. Turn the diagram upside down and knit square 9 between squares 1 and 5, 10 between 9 and 7, 11 between 2 and 9, and 12 between 11 and 10. Now the top has 3 blocks with 4 squares each.

Then knit square 13 next to 6 and 3, 14 next to 10 and 7. Next to square 11 knit a striped right-leaning triangle and a striped left-leaning triangle next to 2. Then continue knitting in the sequence shown on the diagram.

The triangles at the bottom of the cover (43–48) are open top triangles with 27 sts.
Row 1 (WS): K26, p1.
Row 2 (RS): Sl 1 kwise, k11, sl 1, k2tog, psso, k10, p1; turn work and leaving 1 st on the ndl.
Row 3: Sl 1 kwise, k21, p1, turn work, leaving last st on ndl.
Row 4: Sl 1 kwise, k9, sl 1, k2tog, psso, k8, p1, turn work.
Row 5: Sl 1 kwise, k17, p1, turn work.
Row 6: Sl 1 kwise, k7, sl 1, k2tog, psso, k6, p1, turn work.

Row 7: Sl 1 kwise, k14, p1, turn work.

Row 8: Sl 1 kwise, k5, sl 1, k2tog, psso, k4, p1, turn work.

Row 9: Sl 1 kwise, k9, p1, turn work.

Row 10: Sl 1 kwise, k3, sl 1, k2tog, psso, k2, p1, turn work.

Row 11: Sl 1 kwise, k5, p1, turn work.

Row 12: Sl 1 kwise, k1, sl 1, k2tog, psso, p1, turn work.

Row 13: Sl 1 kwise, k1, p1, turn.

Row 14: Sl 1 kwise, sl 1, k1, psso (= 14 sts).

Finish by working 4 rows in stockinette with white in the sts from the bottom triangles.

Finishing

Fold the coffeepot cover into thirds and use it to measure the lining. Use the outline to cut out three pieces in the synthetic lining fabric. Overlap the edges about ¼" (.5 cm) (instead of placing them right sides facing) and sew them together with zigzag stitch. Place the lining into the knitted piece, turning it so that the straight edge is against the wrong side and over the lining; sew edges together. Join the knitted piece and lining with tacking thread here and there and along the opening for the handle with backstitch.

Buttonhole loop: With black, K-CO 12 sts and then BO. Turn the end down and sew it securely to the wrong side, down onto square 36. Sew a button at the corresponding height on the opposite side of the opening. Repeat on the square above.

Loop: With black, K-CO 5 sts and knit a 3⅛" (8 cm) long strip with an edge st at each side. BO and form it into a loop which is then sewn securely to the top of the cover.

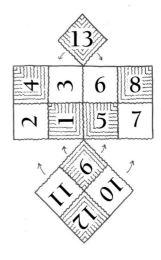

Top

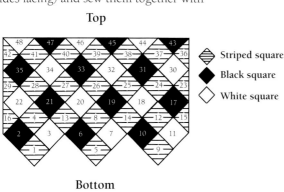

⬦ Striped square

◆ Black square

◇ White square

Bottom

BASKETS FOR A LITTLE OF EVERYTHING

*Y*ou can knit these baskets quickly and use them for a little of everything. Place a glass vase or a glass in the tall basket and use it as a vase or to hold your knitting needles. A small glass in the basket is just right for holding a tea candle.

Design: Eva Jessen

Measurements: Fits a square-bottomed form 2¾" × 2¾" (7 × 7 cm) (after stiffening it fits a one quart/liter milk carton). The height depends on how many rounds you knit. You can change the size on the baskets by knitting more or fewer stitches in the squares and by stretching and stiffening them on larger or smaller bases or something similar. You can use both round and square shapes for forming the baskets.

Yarn: *Fine linen yarn.* Fine cotton thread can also be used.

Color: 3½ oz (100 g) is enough for several baskets.

Needles: Dn 0 (2 mm).

Technique: Basic Square 1, p. 2.

Number of stitches: 25.

Construction: From the center outwards as for Potholder 3, p. 12 and in a ring with the squares standing diamond-

Stiffening Knitted Pieces

Use potato flour. Mix 2 tablespoons potato flour in ½–1 cup (1–2 dl) cold water. Pour it slowly into boiling water, stirring until it has the consistency of paste. Let cool a bit. Place the knitted piece into the stiffening agent so that it becomes thoroughly saturated. Remove it and squeeze out the water. Block it over a form and pin or sew it down. Let it dry completely. Finish by covering with decoupage paste to make the piece totally stiff.

wise on their corner points as for Headband, p. 19.

Gauge (before stiffening): A square should measure 1¾" (4.5 cm) in width and height and 2½" (6.5 cm) diagonally from corner to corner.

Instructions

Bottom (A, B, C, and D): Knit A and B as separate squares. Then knit C in between B and A in the loops of the CO sts and then D between A and B so that the squares are placed like the 4 center squares on Potholder 3.

Next square (E): Begin in the end st of B and pick up and knit 12 sts, working to the left along B, 1 st between B and C and 12 sts along C. Knit square E here. Knit F along C and A in the same way. Then knit squares along A, D, and D, B. Now you should see how the basket is taking form. You have also now knitted a round. From this point, continue knitting in rounds. Each round consists of 4 squares, one in each notch.

Small Basket

Consists of a bottom and 2 rounds (= 12 squares).

Large Basket

Consists of a bottom and 4 rounds (= 20 squares).

Finishing

Backwards crochet along the edges.
Backwards Crochet: Crochet as for single crochet but work from left to right, or "backwards."

Place the basket in the stiffening agent (see "Stiffening" in box, page 46). Then shape the basket over a square or round form. We have used milk cartons here. Hold the corners in position with T-pins or baste in position with sewing thread while the stiffening agent dries.

POT COVER

Yarn: *6-ply jute yarn.*
Needles: 10 (6 mm).

Knitted in the same way as the baskets to the left. The pot cover consists of 1 bottom, 4 squares and then 4 open top triangles, see p. 19. Place the sts on a long piece of yarn (jute yarn is easiest to use) and adjust the width with the yarn.

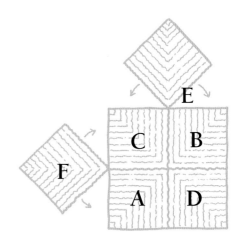

DENIM BACKPACK AND PENCIL CASE

*K*nit this cute denim backpack for a little girl in the family or sew on a wide strap to make it a shoulder bag.

Measurements: The backpack measures 11¾" × 15¼" (30 × 39 cm).

Yarn: *DK weight cotton yarn* Den-M-Knit from Garnstudio.

Colors: 1¾ oz (50 g) dark and 8¾ oz (250 g) light indigo blue.

Needles: Dn 4 (3.5 mm) and 16" (40 cm) circular ndl 4 (3.5 mm).

You will also need a zipper, with a ring, long enough for the opening, a back-pack strap about 1 yd/m long and a peg-shaped button.

Technique: 2-color square.

Number of stitches: 29.

Open top and bottom triangles: See instructions, page 19.

Construction: In a ring with squares standing diamond-wise on their corners as for Headband, p. 19.

Gauge: A square should measure 2¾" (7 cm) in width and height and 4" (10 cm) diagonally from corner to corner.

Diagram: The bag is knitted in one piece, joined in a ring, but the diagram is "spread out." Make a photocopy, cut it out and tape together the sides so that it is easier to understand the bag's construction. Knit the squares in the order indicated by the numbers on the diagram.

Instructions

2-color square

With light blue and dn, K-CO 29 sts.

Row 1 (WS): Knit to last st, p1. Mark the center 3 sts.

Row 2 (RS): Sl 1 kwise, knit to the center 3 sts, sl 1, k2tog, psso, knit to last st, p1.

Row 3: Sl 1 kwise, knit to last st, p1.

Repeat Rows 2 and 3, 2 times, with a decreasing number of sts until there are 4 ridges on RS.

Row 8: Dark yarn—Sl 1 kwise, knit to the 3 center sts, sl—1, k2tog, psso, knit to last st, p1.

Row 9: Sl 1 kwise, purl to end of row.

Row 10: Same as Row 8.

Row 11: Same as Row 9.

Row 12: Light yarn—same as Row 2.

Row 13: Same as Row 3.

Repeat Rows 12 and 13 with a decreasing number of sts, until 3 sts remain.

Next row (WS): Sl 1 kwise, k1, p1.

Next row: Sl 1, k2tog, psso (= 1 st).

Cut yarn, pull tail through sts and pull tight.

Single color square

As for 2-color square, but it is knitted only with light yarn.

Bottom

Squares 1 and 2: Knit 2 separate 2-color squares. Place the squares, with end sts upwards, as shown on the diagram.

Square 3: Single color—Knit square 3 in the notch between squares 1 and 2.

Square 4: Single color—Pick up and knit 14 sts along the top left edge on square 1, go "around the corner" and pick up and knit 1 st in the last CO st on square 1, turn work and K-CO 14 new sts (wavy lines on diagram). Knit square 4 here and cut yarn. Turn work and diagram upside down.

Square 5: Single color—Pick up and knit 14 sts in the loops of CO row along one side of square 4 (wavy lines), 1 st in the corner of square 4 and pick up and knit 14 sts in the CO loops along one side of square 1 (dotted line). Knit a square.

Square 6: Single color—Pick up and knit 14 sts in loops of CO row along one side of square 1 (slash lines), 1 st in corner of square 3 and pick up and knit 14 sts in the CO loops along one side of square 2 (slash lines). Knit a square.

Square 7: Single color—Pick up and knit 14 sts in the CO loops along one side of square 2 (dotted line), knit 1 st in the nearest CO st on the left side of square 2, turn work and K-CO 14 new sts. Knit a square.

Square 8: Single color—Knitted as for square 7 in the same way as square 5 was knitted over square 4.

Front

Back

Bag

You have now knitted the bottom of the backpack and the 1st round. Continue straight up in rounds of 6 squares each following the diagram. Finish with 6 top triangles in the 6 notches.

1 Top Triangle

With light yarn and dn 2 (3 mm), pick up and knit 29 sts as for a square.

Row 1: Sl 1 kwise, k27, p1.

Row 2: Sl 1 kwise, k12, sl 1, k2tog, psso, k11, p1, turn.

Row 3: Sl 1 kwise, k23, p1, turn.

Row 4: Sl 1 kwise, k10, sl 1, k2tog, psso, k9, p1, turn.

Row 5: Sl 1 kwise, K19, p1. turn.

Row 6: Sl 1 kwise, k8, sl 1, k2tog, psso, k7, p1, turn.

Row 7: Sl 1 kwise, k15, p1, turn.

Row 8: Sl 1 kwise, k6, sl 1, k2tog, psso, k5, p1, turn.

Row 9: Sl 1 kwise, k11, p1, turn.

Row 10: Sl 1 kwise, k4, sl 1, k2tog, psso, k3, p1, turn.

Row 11: Sl 1 kwise, k7, p1. turn.

Row 12: Sl 1 kwise, k2, sl 1, k2tog, psso, k1, p1, turn.

Row 13: Sl 1 kwise, k3, p1, turn.

Row 14: Sl 1 kwise, sl 1, k2tog, psso, and place all sts on a holder or waste yarn.

Knit the next 5 triangles in the same way. Do not cut yarn on last triangle, but place all sts on circular ndl 2 (3 mm) and work 6 rows, alternating a purl row with a knit row (reverse stockinette). BO loosely in purl.

Finishing

Spread out backpack as in the diagram and sew a zipper in the opening so that the flap turns downwards. Fold the strap so that it is doubled and sew it securely as shown on the diagram.

Backpack front   **Backpack back**

PENCIL CASE

*Y*ou can easily knit strips for a pencil case
to go in your knapsack or makeup bag.

Measurements: 4¾" × 8¼" (12 × 21 cm).
Yarn: *DK weight cotton yarn.* Den-M-Knit
from Garnstudio.
Colors: 1 ball light and a partial ball dark
indigo blue.
Needles: Dpn and circular ndl 4 (3.5 mm)
and a cable needle.
You will also need an 8" (20 cm) long zip-
per with a ring.
Technique, pattern and joining: As for
Potholder 8, p. 32.
Gauge: The first strip should measure 1¾"
(4.5 cm) in width.

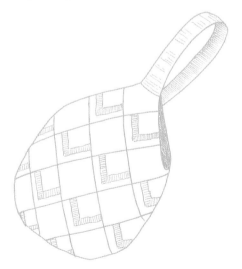

Instructions

Knit the first 3 strips and joining stripes
as for Potholder 8. Only the colors, number of stitches, and length are different.
1st Strip—light blue—10 stitches.
Length: 73 ridges on RS before binding
off—74 ridges/edge sts afterwards
(= 15¾" (40 cm)).

1st joining stripe—dark blue.
Add 2 sts to the 74 (= 76 sts). Knit a
joining stripe on circular ndl.

2nd strip—cables—light blue—9 sts.
2nd joining stripe
As for first joining stripe.

3rd strip—light blue—10 sts.

Finishing

Turn the piece with right sides facing
each other and sew together along the
short side of the 1st strip and on the bottom. Sew a zipper in the opening.

Shoulder Bag

If you want a shoulder bag, CO 10–12
sts and knit a garter stitch piece long
enough to go over the shoulder. Sew it
outside the 2 tips where the zipper begins
and ends so that zipper lies inside the bag.

STAR CAP AND SCARF

*K*nitting caps doesn't need to be boring. Just look at this elegant and different cap formed like a star. A scarf, which is also out of the ordinary, completes the set.

Measurements: Fits most people. The band is adjustable.

Yarn: *Sport weight wool yarn.*

Colors: 1¾ oz (50 g) gray, just under an ounce (25 g) charcoal gray and partial balls of red and red-violet.

Needles: Dn 2 (3 mm), dpn 1 (2.5 mm) and 16" (40 cm) circular ndl 2 (3 mm).

Technique: Basic Squares 1 and 3, pp. 2 and 4.

Number of stitches: 29 and fewer as the work progresses.

Open bottom triangle: p. 19, 29 sts.

Construction: In a ring with squares standing diamond-wise on their corners as for Headband, p. 19.

Pattern: Garter stitch.

Gauge: A 29-stitch square should measure 2⅜" (6 cm) in width and height and 3⅜" (8.5 cm) diagonally from corner to corner.

Instructions

1st round
Color: Charcoal gray, 29 sts.

With charcoal gray, knit 8 squares starting with 29 sts each.

2nd round
Color: Gray, 29 sts.

With gray, knit double squares. On RS, pick up and knit 29 sts along one charcoal gray square in loops of CO sts. Knit a square.

You now have a double square. Repeat until there are 8 double squares.

3rd round
Colors: Red-violet and gray, 25 sts.

Place the double squares with the gray side up so that the corners and end sts point upwards, and then pick up and knit

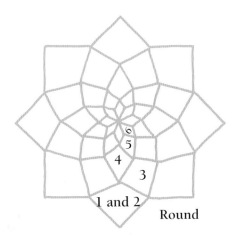

Round

sts in the notches. With red-violet, pick up and knit 14 sts along the top left edge of a square in the gray row, then knit 1 st through both the left corner on one square and the right corner of the next square and pick up and knit 14 sts along the top right edge of this. Knit a square, but on the 1st row, dec 2 sts evenly divided on each side of the center.

Continue working until there are squares in all 7 notches. Bring corners together and then knit a square in the last notch, so that the piece forms a ring.

4th round
Color: Gray, 21 sts.

Knit a square in each of the 8 notches. Begin by picking up and knitting 25 sts and then dec to 21 sts on the first row.

5th round
Color: Gray, 17 sts.

Knit a square in each of the 8 notches. Begin by picking up and knitting 21 sts and then dec to 17 sts on the first row.

6th round
Color: Red, 13 sts.

Knit a square in each of the 8 notches. Begin by picking up and knitting 17 sts and then dec to 13 sts on the first row. Finish with end st-3, but do not cut yarn on the 8th square.

Stalk
Place all 8 sts from the red squares onto a dpn with the last square's end st farthest to the left on the ndl. *Slide sts over to the other end of the ndl, with yarn behind work, pull it and knit all the sts*. Repeat from *-* until the piece is 1¼" (3 cm) long. Then work K2tog across until 2 sts remain. Pass the one st over the other and finish. Weave in ends. Turn the cap upside down and, with gray, knit open bottom triangles in the notches between the charcoal gray squares. Place all sts on circular ndl and work (knit 1 row, purl 1 row) 2 times; at the same time, on row 2, inc to 110–120 sts with incs evenly spaced around. Then work 7 rows in k1, p1 ribbing. BO loosely in ribbing.

SCARF KNITTED IN STRIPS

Measurements: 7½" (19 cm) wide and 71"
(180 cm) long, measured from corner
to corner.
Yarn: *Sport weight wool yarn.*
Colors: A little less than an ounce (25 g)
each red and red-violet, 3½ oz (100 g)
gray.
Needles: Dn and 24" (60 cm) circular ndls
2 (3 mm).
Techniques: Strips, Joining 2, as for
Potholder 6, p. 26.
Pattern: Garter stitch.
Gauge: A strip after joining should meas-
ure 2⅜" (6 cm) wide.

Instructions

1st strip

The strip begins and ends with a
point.
First point: With red-violet and dn, K-CO 2
sts.
*Row 1 (RS): K1, p1.
Row 2 (WS): Sl 1 kwise, M1b (on right
side of st), p1. This first inc is a little
tricky.
Row 3 (RS): Sl 1 kwise, k1, p1.
Row 4 (WS): Sl 1 kwise, M1b, k1, p1
(= 4 sts).
Row 5: Sl 1 kwise, k2, p1.
Row 6: Sl 1 kwise, M1b, k2, p1 (= 5 sts).

Row 7: Sl 1 kwise, k3, p1.
Row 8: Sl 1 kwise, M1b, k3, p1.
Row 9: Sl 1 kwise, k4, p1.
Row 10: Sl 1 kwise, M1b, k4, p1.
Row 11: Sl 1 kwise, k5, p1.
Continue in the same manner, increas-
ing on 1st st after edge st on all WS rows
until there are a total of 15 sts. The last
row is an inc row on WS*.
In-between piece: Change to gray.
Next row (RS): Sl 1 kwise, knit to last st,
p1.
Repeat this row until there are 53 gray
ridges on RS, the last row is worked on
WS.
Last point: Change to red.
Next row (RS): Sl 1 kwise, knit to last st,
p1.
Next row (WS): Sl 1 kwise, knit to last 3
sts, k2tog, p1.
Repeat these 2 rows until 3 sts remain.
Next row: Sl 1 kwise, p2tog.
Next row: Sl 1 kwise, p1.
Next row: Sl 1 kwise, k1, pass slipped st
over the knitted st.
Cut yarn and pull tail through last st.

Joining stripe

With gray yarn and circular ndl, pick up
and knit sts along the right side of the
strip, beginning at the red-violet corner. Go
"around the corner" on the outermost corner and pick up 1 st in the last loop before
the yarn tail, go to the right of the end and
pick up and knit 1 st in every red-violet

edge st, going through both loops (= a total of 15 sts). Then pick up and knit 1 st in all of the gray loops (= 53 sts), but place a marker after 38 sts (of these 53 sts). There should be 68 sts on ndl.

2nd strip

First point: Knit a red corner point as for the 1st strip from * to *. Place the corner's sts on a circular ndl on the red-violet end.

Joining stripe: Change to gray.

Next row (RS): Sl 1 kwise, k13, p2tog (the last red st and the first JSst). Turn work and knit back.

Next row: Sl 1 kwise, knit to last st, p1.

Next row: Sl 1 kwise, k13, p2tog (the last st and the next JSst). Turn work and knit back.

Repeat the last 2 rows until all JSsts have been eliminated, but, when you come to the marker, change to red-violet and dec at the end of all rows from WS as for the 1st strip; at the same time, knitting sts tog with the joining stripe until 3 red sts and 3 gray JSsts remain on WS.

Next row (RS): Sl 1 kwise, k1, p2tog, turn.

Next row: Sl 1 kwise, p2tog.

Next row: Sl 1 kwise, p2tog, turn.

Next row: Sl 1 kwise, p1.

Next row: Sl 1 kwise, k1, pass slipped st over.

Cut yarn and pull tail through last st.

2nd joining stripe

As for first joining stripe.

3rd strip

As for 2nd strip but in the same colors as the first strip. Repeat the 2nd and 3rd strips and the JSst total 19 times, or until the gray yarn is used up.

Squares with a Decreasing Number of Stitches

When you are knitting smaller and smaller squares as the work progresses, you can either pick up fewer stitches in the notch, or pick up as many sts as there are edge sts. Adjust the stitch count on the first row, so that there is 1 st in the center and an equal number sts on each side of center st.

WRISTWARMERS

W ristwarmers are "in" and these are especially lovely. The pattern develops as the squares are knitted. The beads are strung on a thread and knitted in after each stitch. Imagine these wristwarmers as the edging under a long-sleeved black sweater or as cuffs with the points turned up towards a pair of gloves.

Measurements: Circumference 8¼"
(21 cm), length 4½" (11.5 cm).
If you want smaller wristwarmers, knit the squares with fewer stitches and fewer beads.
Yarn: *Fingering weight wool yarn.*
Color: partial skein of black.
You will also need a little packet of small copper beads, a thin sewing or beading needle and sewing thread for stringing the beads onto the yarn.
Needles: 0 (2 mm).
Technique: Basic Square 1, p. 2, with beads.
Number of Stitches: 19.
Open top and bottom triangles: See instructions below.
Construction: In a ring with squares standing diamond-wise on their corners as for the Headband, p. 19.
Pattern: Garter stitch.
Gauge: A square should measure max 1" (2.7 cm) in width and height and 1⅝"

(4.2 cm) diagonally from corner to corner.

Instructions

1st round
String 28 beads onto the yarn. Knit a Basic Square 1, but, on row 3 (WS), knit in 16 beads, 1 bead after each st except for the last st. On row 7, knit in 12 beads. Knit a total of 5 squares and place them "hand in hand" with the end sts upwards.

2nd round
Now knit 4 squares in the notches. For each of these squares, use 32 beads. On Row 1, knit in 18 beads and on Row 5, 14 beads. Form the piece into a ring, so that the 1st and 5th squares from the 1st round go "hand in hand", and knit the 5th square in the last notch.

3rd round
Knit 5 squares, one in each notch, and knit in 18 beads on Row 1 on each of the squares.

4th and 5th rounds
Knit squares without beads in all the notches.

6th round
Knit 1 top triangle of 19 sts in each notch.

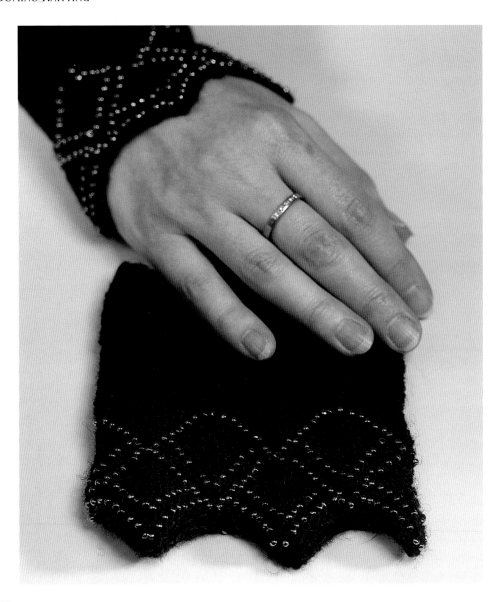

Row 1 (WS): K18, p1.

Row 2 (RS): Sl 1 kwise, k7, sl 1, k2tog, psso, k6, p1, turn work, leaving 1 st on ndl.

Row 3: Sl 1 kwise, k13, p1, turn work, leaving 1 st on ndl.

Row 4: Sl 1 kwise, k5, sl 1, k2tog, psso, k4, p1, turn work.

Row 5: Sl 1 kwise, k9, p1, turn.

Row 6: Sl 1 kwise, k3, sl 1, k2tog, psso, k2, p1, turn work.

Row 7: Sl 1 kwise, k5, p1, turn.

Row 8: Sl 1 kwise, k1, sl 1, k2tog, psso, p1, turn.

Row 9: Sl 1 kwise, k1, p1, turn.

Row 10: Sl 1, k1, psso (= 10 sts).

Ribbed edging

Divide all the sts from the top triangles evenly onto 4 dpn 0 (2 mm) and work 6 rows K1, p1 ribbing; at the same time, on row 1, decrease evenly around to 56 sts. BO in ribbing.

Stringing Beads onto Yarn

Double the sewing thread and thread the two ends through the eye of the needle. Hitch the thread to the yarn and string the beads onto the sewing or bead needle and then over to the yarn. The sewing thread can then be removed from the yarn.

FLOWER CAPS FOR CHILDREN AND ADULTS

*Y*ou can become obsessed with knitting these wonderful caps. There are two styles of cap, one with a rolled edge and the other with an upturned triangle edging. The cap with the triangle edging is sized only for adults.

Size: Child (adult).

Measurements: The cap's circumference is about 19¾" (50 cm) (20½" [52 cm)]) and is very elastic.

Yarn: *Sport weight wool yarn.*

Colors: The cap can be knitted in two shades like a checkerboard with a third color on top or in tone-on-tone berry colors with a green top.

Needles: Dn 2 (3 mm). For a rolled edging, use a 16" (40 cm) circular ndl 2 (3 mm). 2 dpn 1 (2.5 mm) for the stalk.

Technique: Basic Square 1, p. 2.

Number of stitches: See instructions, page 65.

Open bottom triangle: 23 (25 sts).

Construction: In a ring with squares standing diamond-wise on their corners as for Headband, p. 19.

Gauge: A square of 25 sts should measure 1¾" (4.5 cm) in width and height and 2½" (6.5 cm) diagonally from corner to corner.

Border: Rolled edge.

CAP WITH TRIANGLE EDGE

NOTE: Only adult size.

Instructions

Turned-up triangle edge

First knit a round with 7 blocks consisting of 3 small joined squares each.

1st square—A

With dn, K-CO 13 sts. Knit a Basic Square 1 but change color after the 1st row and knit the rest of the square with the second color.

2nd square—B

As for square A. Place B next to A with the corners downwards as in the drawing.

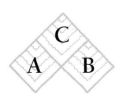

3rd square—C

Knit a single color square C over A and B. Now you have a block which consists of 3 small squares. Knit a total of 7 such blocks. Place this in front of you with the 2 corners downwards as in the drawing, and align the blocks "hand in hand."

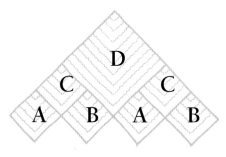

Knit a large single color square D with 25 sts in each notch between the 7 blocks. Form the piece into a ring, so that the 2 outermost corners are "hand in hand." Knit a 7th square in the notch which remains. The piece is now a joined ring, and the turned-up cuff is finished. Turn piece so WS is facing out.

1st round: Knit a square with 25 sts in each of the 7 notches from the triangle edge.

2nd round: As for the 1st round, but with 23 sts.

3rd round: As for the 1st round, but with 21 sts. Continue in rounds with 2 sts fewer in the squares, as follows:

4th round: 19 sts.

5th round: 17 sts.

6th round: 15 sts.

7th round: 13 sts.

Do not cut yarn on last square.

Stalk

Place all the end sts from the squares in the 7th round onto a dpn. Knit a stalk for the top on 2 dpn, first knit 1 row over all the sts; do not turn work but slide all the sts to the other end of ndl; bring yarn behind work and pull to tighten. Knit another row. Continue in this manner until the stalk measures ¼–1¼" (2–3 cm).

Next row: (K2 tog) 3 times, K1 (= 4 sts). K2tog, K2tog, pass one stitch over the other and finish off. Sew seams between each square on last round if desired.

CAP WITH ROLLED EDGE

For both child and adult sizes.

Instructions

1st round: Knit 6 (7) single color squares
with 23 (25) sts.
2nd round: 23 (23) sts.
3rd round: 21 (21) sts.
4th round: 19 (19) sts.
5th round: 17 (17) sts.
6th round: 15 (15) sts.
7th round: 13 (13) sts.

Stalk: Same as for the stalk on the cap
with triangle edging.

Open bottom triangles

Turn the cap upside down and knit
open bottom triangles (see below) with
23 (25) sts (as for Headband, p. 19) in
each of the 6 (7) notches. Place the sts
from the triangles onto a waste yarn for
the rolled edge.

Open bottom triangle, 23 sts.

Row 1 (WS): K22, p1.
Row 2 (RS): Sl 1 kwise, k9, sl 1, k2tog,
psso, k8, p1, turn work leaving 1 st on
ndl.
Row 3: Sl 1 kwise, k17, p1, turn work
leaving 1 st on ndl.
Row 4: Sl 1 kwise, k7, sl 1, k2tog, psso,
k6, p1, turn.
Row 5: Sl 1 kwise, k13, p1, turn.
Row 6: Sl 1 kwise, 5, sl 1, k2tog, psso, k4,
p1, turn.
Row 7: Sl 1 kwise, k9, p1, turn work.
Row 8: Sl 1 kwise, k3, sl 1, k2tog, psso,
k2, p1, turn.
Row 9: Sl 1 kwise, k5, p1, turn.
Row 10: Sl 1 kwise, k1, sl 1, k2tog, psso,
p1, turn.
Row 11: Sl 1 kwise, k1, p1, turn.
Row 12: Sl 1, k1, psso (= 12 sts).

Simple rolled edge

Knit 14 rows in the round (= stockinette), but, on Row 2, inc to about 90
(105) sts, with incs evenly divided around.
BO loosely. Let the edging roll up.

VEST FOR MOTHER AND BABY AND A PONCHO

*H*ere are the instructions for exciting, easy *and* and unusual garments knitted with squares: a wide vest for a woman which can easily be knitted in larger sizes and a matching vest for baby. In addition, there is an elegant poncho which can also be used as a shawl under or over a coat. In short, a garment with many possibilities.

Most of the squares are garter stitch and single color, but the vest has a section with patterned squares. Before you start to knit, choose which pattern you prefer: "wings," as on the baby vest, or "spots."

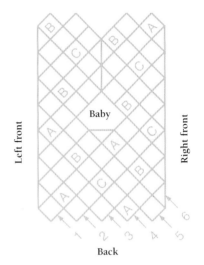

Baby

Left front

Right front

Back

BABY VEST

Size: One size. If you want a larger size baby vest, knit larger squares. Remember to increase the number of stitches in the border to correspond.

Width: 12½" (32 cm).
Length: 9½" (24 cm).
Yarn: *Wool Baby yarn.*
Colors: 2 balls red = main color and a little orange (A), yellow (B), and pink (C). If you knit a larger size vest, you will need more yarn.
Needles: Dn and circular ndls 1 (2.5 mm).

Technique: Basic Squares 1 (single color) and 3 ("wings") or 4 ("spots"), pp. 2 and 4–5.
Number of stitches: 23.
Right- and left-leaning triangles: 12 sts. See p. 19.
Construction: Diagonal panels as for Potholder 4, p. 15.
Details: Pompons, see sidebar on page 68.
Gauge: A square should measure 1½" (4 cm) in width and height and 2⅜" (6 cm) diagonally from corner to corner.

WOMAN'S VEST
Size: One width, 4 lengths.
Width: 37" (94 cm).
Length: 21⅞" (25¼", 28⅛", 32") [55, 64, 72, 81 cm].

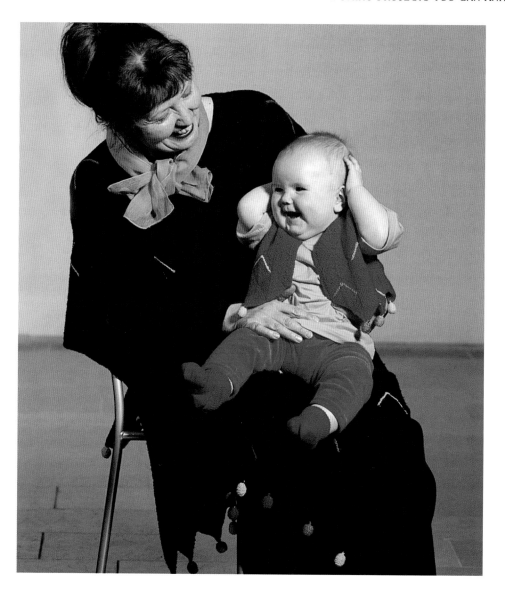

Yarn: *Sport weight wool yarn.*

Colors: 400 (450) 500 (550) g Main Color (MC) and 15 g each of 3 pattern colors (A, B, and C).

Needles: Dn and circular ndls 2 (3 mm).

Technique: Basic Squares 1 (single color) and 3 ("wings") or 4 ("spots"), pp. 2 and 4–5.

Number of stitches: 29.

Right- and left-leaning triangles: 15 sts. See p. 19.

Construction: Diagonal panels as for Potholder 4, p. 15.

Details: Pompons, see below.

Gauge: A square should measure 2⅜" (6 cm) in width and height and 3⅜" (8.5 cm) diagonally from corner to corner.

Knitted Pompon

With ndl 2 (3 mm), K-CO 10 sts, leaving a tail of about 19½" (50 cm).

Work 7 rows in stockinette (alternating 1 row knit and 1 row purl). Do not BO but measure about 1½ yds/m yarn before you cut yarn. Thread short tail through tapestry needle and draw through the loops of the 10 CO sts; pull sts together; and sew the piece into a little bag with wrong side facing out. The top part is sewn together rather loosely. Then draw the needle through the sts on the knitting needle and let it hang loose. Bundle the long yarn end into a neat little skein and stuff it into the bag, tighten the loose part of the seam and draw out the thread. Sew the pompon securely to the garment, twist the yarn around the needle a couple of times and then sew, as invisibly as possible, up and down through the pompon a couple of times and then fasten in the yarn. *NOTE:* If you are putting pompons onto baby clothes, be extra careful to fasten the pompons well, so they can't be tugged off.

PONCHO, VEST, SCARF

Size: One size.

Width: 37" (94 cm).

Length: 38½" (98 cm) measured at center back and 32" (81 cm) from the front.

Yarn: *Sport weight wool yarn.*

Colors: 550 g Main color (MC) and 25 g each of 3 pattern colors (A, B, and C).

Needles, technique, number of stitches, triangles: See "Woman's Vest."

Construction: A combination of straight panels worked starting at the bottom and diagonal panels as for Potholders 2 and 4, pp. 9 and 15.

Detail: Pompons, p. 68.

Gauge: See "Woman's Vest."

Square 4, with "spots"

K-CO 23 (29) sts and knit as for Basic Square 1, but, when 9 (13) sts remain, on a RS row, change to the color noted on the diagram and knit the rest of the square with that color.

CHANGING SIZES

You can change a size on a domino design knitted with squares simply by making the squares smaller or larger. This will change both the height and width.

LEFTOVER YARN

Domino knitting is an ideal way to use up leftover yarns. For example, use them to knit a sweater with striped squares. TIP: Choose one color and use it as one of the colors on every square. That makes a calming background so that you can use as many other colors as you want in the squares without the sweater looking too garish.

Women's Vest

Left front

Right front

Back

BABY/WOMAN'S VEST AND PONCHO

Diagram: Follow the diagram. There are diagrams for the baby vest, woman's vest, and the poncho.

Woman's vest: The entire diagram shows the largest vest which consists of 18 triangles on each side, the next largest has 16 triangles, the next 14, and the shortest 12.

All Garments: The blank squares in the diagram are Basic Square 1, knitted with MC and squares with A, B, and C are Basic Squares 3 or 4, which are knitted with MC in either "wings" or "spot" pattern in the color indicated on the diagram.

Colors: For these instructions, I've used 3 colors for "wings" or "spots." Of course, you can use more or fewer colors if you wish. I suggest that you make a photocopy of the diagram and color in the squares with the colors you want.

Back and Front

Poncho

Follow the diagram and knit the first 3 squares in panels 1, 2, and 3 (9 squares altogether) as for Potholder 2 and measure the gauge. Finish working panel 1, then panel 2, etc. The last block in panel 1 is a left-leaning triangle and the first block in the 12th panel is a right-leaning triangle.

Baby and woman's vest

Choose the size and begin with panel 1. Then work the 2nd panel, 3rd panel, etc. Work following the diagram. Measure the center square when the 3rd panel is finished. The 2nd block in the 1st panel is a left-leaning triangle. The first block in the 6th (baby)/12th (woman's) panel is a right-leaning triangle.

Finishing—Baby Vest

Borders: With red, pick up and knit sts along the front edges, front and back neck (11 sts for each triangle and 1 st for each

Seaming with Mattress Stitch

Seam pieces together on the right side with mattress stitch, which makes an almost invisible seam.

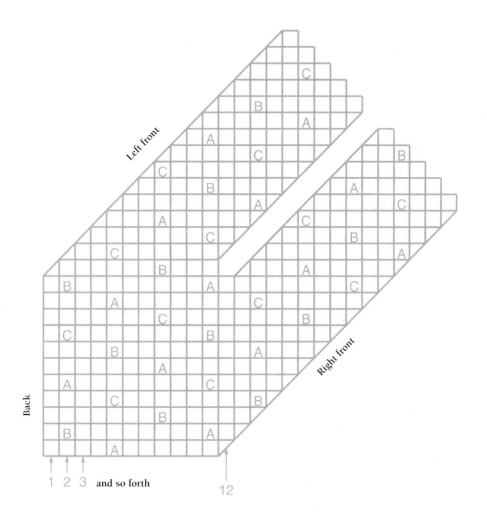

Left front

Back

Right front

1 2 3 and so forth

12

edge st in the neck). Knit 3 rows and inc 1 st in the corner of the V-neck on RS. BO loosely.

Work the borders on each side along the triangles in the same way. Sew together 1½ triangles in each side starting at the bottom. Make 9 pompons using only one yard/meter yarn in each and sew them absolutely securely to each corner at the bottom as the first thing a baby will do is put these pompons into the mouth.

Finishing—Woman's vest

Borders: With MC, pick up and knit sts along the front edges and around the neck (20 sts for each triangle and 1 st for each edge st on back neck). Knit 2 rows and BO loosely on WS.

Work edges in the same way on each side along the triangles. Sew together 3 (4) 5 (6) triangles on each side, starting at the bottom. Then make 21 pompons and sew them securely at the corners on the bottom.

Finishing—Poncho

You don't need to knit borders on the poncho. Make 13 pompons and sew them securely on the corners of the front and in 3 of the corners on the back.

SOUL-WARMING SHRUG

T he shrug has had a renaissance—and it is so sweet in assorted pastels. The squares on the sleeves decrease in size as one works from shoulder to wrist, and in this way, the sleeves are automatically shaped.

Size: One size.

Measurements: 58½" (148 cm) from wrist to wrist.

Yarn: *Sport weight yarn.*

Colors: Gray-rose (A), rose (B), yellow-rose (C), khaki (D), yellow-green (E), and green (F). 1¾ oz (50 g) of each color.

Needles: Dn and circular ndls 2 (3mm). Dpn 2 (3 mm) for the cuffs.

Technique: Basic square 1, page 2.

Number of stitches: 29 and then gradually smaller as one works down the sleeve.

Construction: Diagonal panels on the front and back as for Potholder 4, page 15. Squares on the sleeves are arranged circularly with squares meeting at the corners as on the Headband, page 19.

Details: Pompons, page 68.

Gauge: Square D should measure 2⅜" (6 cm) in width and height and 3⅜" [8.5 cm)]) diagonally from corner to corner.

Instructions

First knit a gauge swatch as shown in the drawing with panel 1 (at the arrow "1" under the diagram), which consists of 2 squares of 29 sts with colors F and B; panel 2 has 3 squares and the 3rd panel has 4 squares. Measure the gauge on the middle square, knitted with color B. If gauge is correct, continue working. The gauge swatch is the starting point for panels 1, 2, and 3 on the chart.

Back and Front

Knit the rest of the back and front (= the center section marked off by dark lines on the diagram, panels 1–5.) All the squares start with 29 sts; colors are indicated on the diagram.

Left Sleeve

Round 1: 27 sts—turn the work and diagram, so that the side with the number

Gauge Swatch

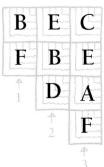

75

29 on the diagram (= back) points to the left and "Front" points right. The direction of knitting changes, (see drawing, where the yellow squares are turned in the new direction). See "begin sleeve" on the diagram. Knit the center 4 squares in the 4 notches. Then knit the outer right square at "begin sleeve" with color E as follows: K-CO 13 sts, pick up and knit 1 st in the outermost corner of the square knitted with color A (at the end st) and then pick up and knit 14 sts along square A. Next, knit the square at far left with color F as follows: Pick up and knit 13 sts along the square on the back, knit 1 st in the corner of the first square in panel 1, turn the work and K-CO 13 sts. Knit a square.

Round 2: 27 sts—Join the piece so that the first and last squares in this row go "hand in hand" (E and F on the

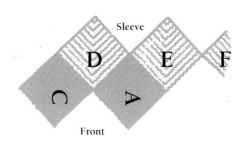

One square with color A

One square with color B

One square with color C

One square with color D

One square with color E

One square with color F

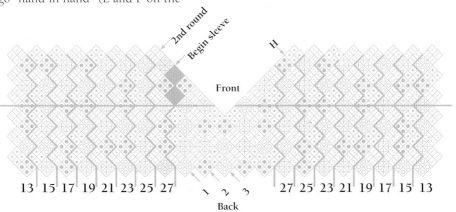

drawing). Knit a square in each notch all the way around. Continue knitting in the round in the same way (as for the Headband) with fewer sts. See the number of sts on the left side of the chart. In this way, the sleeve is shaped and becomes narrower as one works down. To finish, knit a round of bottom triangles with color E in the notches at the bottom of each sleeve as follows:

Pick up and knit 13 sts in a notch.

Row 1: Sl 1 kwise, k11, p1, turn work, leaving last st on ndl.

Row 2: Sl 1 kwise, k4, sl 1, k2tog, psso, k3, p1, turn work, leaving last sts on ndl.

Row 3: Sl 1 kwise, k7, p1, turn.

Row 4: Sl 1 kwise, k2, sl 1 k2tog, psso, k1, p1, turn.

Row 5: Sl 1 kwise, k3, p1, turn.

Row 6: Sl 1 kwise, sl 1, k2tog, psso, k3tbl (= 7 sts).

Continue knitting triangles in the same way, with each triangle to the left of the previous one. Work around until you have a total of 6 triangles. Continue, using dpn, placing 14 sts onto each of 3 ndls (= 42 sts) and knit stockinette in the round (knit every row). Knit 12 rows and BO loosely. Weave in any loose ends and let the edging roll up.

Knit the other sleeve in the same way using the colors as indicated on the chart.

Rolled edging

With color B, circular ndl, and beginning at H on the chart, pick up and knit sts along the squares in the V on the front. Finish at the yellow square with 4 x's in it. Working back and forth, knit 1 row (WS). The first row is knitted on RS; dec evenly across row so that there are 12 sts per square and 1 extra st at each end (= 146 sts). Then work 8 more rows in stockinette and BO loosely. Weave in any loose ends. Let edging roll. Knit 1 pompon with color A, 2 with color B and 2 with color C, and sew them to the 5 corners on the back.

STRIPED SHAWL

*L*ay this shawl decoratively over your
shoulders or drape it around the neck as
*an exciting scarf with stairstep edges. Notice
that the stripes run across on the front and
lengthwise on the back.*

Size: One size.

Measurements: 63" (160 cm) for the
longest strip and 29½" (75 cm) at the
center.

Yarn: *Sport weight wool yarn.*

Colors 13 oz (350 g) marine-blue (M), 1
oz (25 g) each red-violet (R), lemon (S),
gray-green (G), olive (O), beige (B), and
ice-blue (I).

Needles: 32" or 40" (80 or 100 cm) long
circular ndl 2 (3 mm) and 2 dpn size 2
(3 mm) for the I-cord border.

Technique: Strips. Joining 2, Potholder 6,
p. 26.

Pattern: Garter stitch in stripes.

Gauge: 24 sts and 26 ridges (= 52 rows)
= 4" × 4" (10 × 10 cm) in garter st.

First Strip

Follow the diagram. Arrow 1 shows
where the 1st strip begins. With red-violet
and dpn 2 (3 mm) or dn, K-CO 30 sts.
Row 1 (RS): K29, p1.
Row 2: Sl 1 kwise, k28, p1.
Row 3: Marine-blue, Sl 1 kwise, k28, p1.
Row 4: Sl 1 kwise, k28, p1.

Row 5: Red-violet, Sl 1 kwise, k28, p1.
Repeat Rows 2–5 until there are 8 red-
violet ridges with 7 marine-blue ridges in
between (a total of 15 ridges). Now you
have knitted a striped block (R). Now
knit 25 marine-blue ridges (= the blank
square on the diagram). Continue, alternately knitting striped and plain marine-
blue blocks, following the diagram.

Finish with beige after 11 striped and
10 marine-blue blocks. BO on RS after
the 8th beige stripe on the 11th striped
block.

1st joining stripe

Place the 1st strip as on the diagram
with the red-violet end (CO row) turned
towards you and RS facing. Skip over the
red-violet striped block, count 5 ridges
up in the first marine-blue block along
the first strip and place a marker between
the 5th and 6th ridges. With marine-blue
and circular ndl, pick up and knit 1 st in
each edge st along the 1st strip's right
side. Begin at the marker.

After 16 sts, place a marker (5 ridges
before a colored block), *pick up and
knit 25 sts (along 5 marine-blue ridges),
place a marker, pick up and knit 15 sts
(along 5 ridges on both side of the 15 sts
in the marine-blue block), place a marker
*. Repeat from *-* and finish with 16 sts;
the 16th st is 4 ridges before the last
striped block (= 377 sts). Cut yarn. Be
sure that the number of sts between the

markers is correct, so that there are exactly 25 sts along the marine-blue blocks and 15 sts along the striped blocks. It is absolutely necessary that the stitch count be correct; otherwise the stripes will not match.

2nd strip

Use the first st in the joining stripe as the beg st and K-CO 30 sts with beige extending out from the joining stripe (= 377 marine-blue and 30 beige sts on ndl).

Row 1: K29, p2tog (the last beige st with the first marine-blue st on the joining stripe), turn work.

Row 2: Sl 1 kwise, k28, p1.

Row 3: Marine-blue, Sl 1 kwise, k28, p3tog, turn.

Row 4: Sl 1 kwise, k28, p1.

Row 5: Beige, Sl 1 kwise, k28, p2 tog, turn.

Row 6: Sl 1 kwise, k28, p1.

Row 7: Marine-blue, Sl 1 kwise, k28, p2tog. turn.

Repeat Rows 4–7 until the first striped block is finished. Continue, following the diagram and joining on the left side until all JSsts are eliminated, and you have knitted 10 striped and 9 marine-blue blocks. Continue joining the 2nd strip with the first in this way.

BO on RS and, at the same time, purling the last st tog with the last marine-blue st from the joining stripe and bind it off.

2nd joining stripe

Knitted as the first joining stripe and begun as it was between the 5th and 6th ridge (20 ridges up). Pick up and knit a total of 337 sts.

3rd Strip

As for 2nd strip; begin with gray-green.

3rd joining stripe

As for 2nd joining stripe, 297 sts.

4th Strip

As for 2nd strip; begin with red-violet.

4th joining stripe

As for 2nd joining stripe, 257 sts.

5th Strip

As for 2nd strip; begin with beige.

5th joining stripe

As for 2nd joining stripe, 217 sts.

6th Strip

As for 2nd strip; begin with gray-green.

Finishing

Weave in all loose ends.

I-cord Border

Knit an I-cord with 4 sts along the longest side with color M.

Garter Stitch Edge

Along the stairsteps and the straight side at the back, knit a garter stitch border. Begin where you finished the I-cord on RS. With marine-blue and circular ndl 2 (3 mm) (you will need several circular needles), pick up and knit 30 sts along the CO row on the 1st strip, 21 sts along the side (1 st in each edge st), 30 sts along the 2nd strip, 21 sts in the side, 30 sts along the 3rd strip, etc. On the long side without the I-cord, pick up and knit 1 st in each edge st, through both loops, and, along the last stairstep side, pick up and knit 30 sts in the 6th strip along the BO row, 21 sts on the side, 30 sts along the 5th strip, etc. Knit 1 row over all sts and BO loosely.

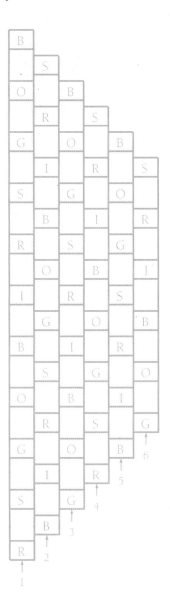

DESIGN YOUR OWN DOMINO SWEATER

Now that you have learned the Domino knitting techniques, you are ready to make your own pattern and try a little larger project. How would it be to work out your own design for a sweater? The information below guides you through the process.

It is possible to design by knitting together squares and strips haphazardly, but it is easiest to sketch and count a little first.

Start with a sweater which fits well and use it as the **pattern**. Measure and draw it on graph paper. For example, 4 × 4 squares = 4" (10 cm). Write out the measurements on a measuring sketch.

Decide if you want to knit **strips** or **squares**—or a combination.

If you want to knit **squares**, you must decide if they will lie in vertical panels or with the points up, diamond-wise. If you want to knit **strips**, you should decide on the pattern and width of the strips.

The **colors** are important, so here is some advice to help. Put a basket with the colors you want to have in your next project in the living room. Let the basket sit out for several days. Walk around the colors and, if some color seems wrong, take it out and put in another color. Often one goes by the yarns without

Washing Wool

Wool garments don't need to be washed too often, because wool has self-cleaning properties. Instead, hang the garment outside on a dry day to air out for a couple of hours. If there are spots on the garment, you can wash it by hand in a large tub of water and special wool washing soap. Be sure that you use the same temperature water for washing and rinsing. It is better to wash in water that is too cool than water which is too hot. Centrifuge or spin the garment in the washing machine, spread it out to the correct measurements and hang it up on a broad pole. Shake it a bit whenever you go by so that it regains the natural bounce and spring of wool. If you don't have a centrifuge, you can quickly squeeze (not wring) out as much water as possible. Lay the garment out on a handtowel and let it dry flat.

really looking at them but suddenly sees how it ought to be.

Always decide first how the **neckline** should look.

Knit a gauge swatch with the yarn you are thinking of using. Measure the gauge, that is, the width, height and diagonal of a square, the width on a strip and perhaps also how many stitches and rows there are in 4" (10 cm).

Draw the garment on graph paper—and remember to begin with the neckline! Maybe there is something which doesn't work with your idea. You can redo the sketch or change the sizes of the squares, and, of course, you must knit a new swatch. Designing takes reworking several times in order to reach the desired result. So don't worry, fight on.

YARN

Before you begin to knit, you need to get the right yarn. Under "Yarn" at the beginning of each pattern, it tells you which yarn was used in the actual model.

Pressing, Or?

You have now finished making a garment but there is a little care which needs to be done before you can wear it. Begin by verifying exactly what kind of material you have, than decide on the proper finishing method. Yarn companies must always be sure that the yarn has what it promises, therefore the handling they recommend should always be carefully considered. Always read the yarn label or pattern instructions. Often the label says handwash and no ironing. However, I dare to say that most qualities of wool yarn (except superwash) can be ironed. I don't mean that the work should be pressed flat, but, holding a steam iron a little bit above the piece, you can smooth the work with your hands and spread it out into the correct shape. Be sure that you don't burn your hands with the steam! I don't have much experience with superwash and synthetic fibers, so you should try these yourself. Always use the gentlest way first. Make sure it hasn't caused any harm before you dare take the next step. I would always keep the steam iron totally away from these materials. Instead, dampen the pieces, stretch them out into correct form and block them to measurements.

It also says, for example, *sport weight wool yarn*. Refer to the Resource and Yarn List on page 86 for yarn sources and substitutions.

Not all fine wool yarns have the same thickness. Knit a swatch so that you can be certain that the yarn you have chosen is suitable for the pattern. Many of the garments in this book are knitted with Scottish or Shetland Tweed (225m/50g or 150 yds/oz), which is spun by a tweed spinnery in Scotland from a very fine wool. All of the models can be made with other colors than those shown in the book. The yarn kits are packaged in a bag with yarn, instructions, and picture. In the chart on page 86, you can see the names of yarn and yarn shops. If you use another yarn than that recommended in the instructions, keep in mind that the yardage can vary.

GAUGE

The gauge determines how large your piece will be. If you are knitting the shrug on p. 75, it is very important that you get the exact gauge, but if you knit the poncho on p. 66, it is not as important. No matter what you do, you must knit a gauge swatch before you begin knitting.

SQUARES

If, for example, you have knitted a gauge swatch for the shawl on p. 37, and the square is larger or smaller than the size specified in the pattern, you can do the following:

1 use smaller or larger needles
2 use finer or heavier yarn
3 use fewer or more stitches per square
4 knit fewer or more squares in the length and width.

The squares are practical because, if you want to make the piece smaller than you had thought about at the beginning, you can knit squares 2 sts smaller. In that way, the piece will be smaller in both length and width.

STRIPS

If you are knitting strips and have fewer or more stitches that you had planned on, you can try recommendations 1 or 2 above. You could also use fewer or more stitches per strip or knit the strips shorter or longer.

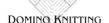

SUPPLIES AND EQUIPMENT

Vivian invites you to visit her website at www.viv.dk.

Many of the specific yarns and kits for these projects are available through the following U.S. shops:

Neitzie's Nook
225 Mill St.
Bristol, PA 19007
www.neitzienook.com

Yarn Expressions
7914 S. Memorial Pkwy #B4
Huntsville, AL 35802
www.onefineyarn.com

The following shops or distributors supply some of the yarns used in the patterns or carry a yarn that you can easily substitute:

fine wools, sportweight wools, dk wool and cottons, fine and heavy linen
Crystal Palace Yarns
a division of Straw Into Gold, Inc.
2320 Bissell Ave.
Richmond, CA 94804
(510) 237-9988 fax (510) 237-9809
www.straw.com

baby wool, baby cotton, dk wool and cotton, sportweight wool
Dale of Norway
N16 W23390 Stoneridge Dr., Ste. A
Waukesha, WI 53188
(800) 441-dale
www.dale.no

baby wool, dk wool and cotton, denim cotton, sportweight wool
Rowan
5 Northern Blvd.
Amherst, NH 03031
(603) 886-5041
e-mail wfibers@aol.com
www.knitrowan.com

Garnstudio/Aurora Yarns
PO Box 3068
Moss Beach, CA 94038
(650) 728-2730 fax (650) 728-8539
e-mail aurorayarns@pacbell.net
www.garnstudio.com

fine wools
Schoolhouse Press
Jamieson & Smith Shetland Wool
6899 Cary Bluff
Pittsville, WI 54466
(800) 968-5648
Jamieson & Smith
www.shetland-wool-brokers.zetnet.co.uk

Domino needles are available through:
Woodland Woolworks
PO Box 850
Carlton, OR 97111
(503) 852-7376 orders (800) 547-3725
info@woolworks.com

ABBREVIATIONS

The abbreviations used in this book are listed below. Some of the abbreviations are explained in another place in the book. Go to the page indicated for more information about the technique; see, for example, M1b on page 38.

beg	=	begin
beg st	=	beginning stitch = the stitch used for starting the knitted cast-on. It can be a whole new stitch which is cast on, a stitch which is already on the needle, or a loop in the work; see page 40.
BO	=	bind off (British cast off)
CC	=	contrast color
cm	=	centimeter(s)
CO	=	cast-on
dec	=	decrease
dn	=	domino needle
dpn	=	double-pointed needles (British double-ended needles)
end st	=	end stitch, see page 5
fig	=	figure
g	=	gram(s)
inc	=	increase
JS	=	joining stripe
JSst	=	joining stripe stitch
K	=	knit
K-CO	=	knitted cast-on, see page 4.
K2tog	=	knit two together
m	=	meter(s)
M1b	=	make 1 in stitch below, see page 38.
MC	=	main color
mkr	=	marker
mm	=	millimeter(s)
ndl	=	needle
oz	=	ounce(s)
P	=	purl
P2tog	=	purl 2 together
RS	=	right side
sl 1 kwise	=	slip one st as if to knit
sl 1 pwise	=	slip one as if to purl
sl 1, K1, psso	=	slip one, knit one, pass slip st over
sl 1, K2tog, psso	=	slip one, knit two together, pass slip st over
st	=	stitch
tog	=	together
WS	=	wrong side

INDEX